Narrative Based Ev-¹

"Dr. Harrison presents a new way of ⬛⬛⬛⬛⬛⬛⬛⬛⬛ xploring deeply into the storied lives of her s ⬛⬛⬛⬛⬛⬛ ⬛r. Her new approach impacts the educational pro⬛ ⬛⬛⬛ ⬛sitions to re-think curricula designs for the twenty-first cen

Robert C⬛ ⬛rofessor of Secondary Education,
Arizona State University

"In this insightful volume, Marsha Dianne Harrison has brought us a realistic way of evaluating learning through 'narrative based evaluation.' I can't think of a better way to assess outcomes of a writing curriculum than through narrative based evaluation. Dr. Harrison uses autobiography, biography, and story to enlighten our assessment processes. In a very significant way, she gives us opportunity to learn narrative based evaluation by evaluating her worn work as a writer, teacher, and researcher. This book will be of great assistance to qualitative, interpretive, arts-based, and mytho-poetic teachers, researchers, and writers."

Nelson L. Haggerson, Jr., Professor Emeritus,
Arizona State University

"This book reveals the power of narrative to transform and heal in an educational setting. Thus, educators in particular will find an alternative way of being *teacher*. Dr. Harrison invites teachers to see themselves as companions on the journey to understanding self and curriculum, to write so as to come to know themselves and others. However, the stories of personal reflection, growth, and courage provide inspiration for readers of any profession. Dr. Harrison writes with authenticity, sincerity, and warmth, inviting readers to wander with her as she explores the potency and potential of narrative based evaluation."

Mary Beth Spore, Assistant Professor of English,
University of Pittsburgh at Greensburg

Narrative Based Evaluation

COUNTERPOINTS

Studies in the
Postmodern Theory of Education

Joe L. Kincheloe and Shirley R. Steinberg
General Editors

Vol. 185

PETER LANG
New York · Washington, D.C./Baltimore · Bern
Frankfurt am Main · Berlin · Brussels · Vienna · Oxford

Marsha Dianne Harrison

Narrative Based Evaluation

Wording Toward the Light

PETER LANG
New York · Washington, D.C./Baltimore · Bern
Frankfurt am Main · Berlin · Brussels · Vienna · Oxford

Library of Congress Cataloging-in-Publication Data

Harrison, Marsha Dianne.
Narrative based evaluation: wording toward the light / Marsha Dianne Harrison
p. cm. — (Counterpoints; vol. 185)
Includes bibliographical references.
1. Storytelling—Therapeutic use. 2. Personal construct therapy—Case studies.
3. Narration (Rhetoric)—Psychological aspects. I. Title.
II. Counterpoints (New York, N.Y.); vol. 185.
RC489.S74 H37   616.89'1—dc21   00-049732
ISBN 0-8204-5274-2
ISSN 1058-1634

Die Deutsche Bibliothek-CIP-Einheitsaufnahme

Harrison, Marsha Dianne:
Narrative based evaluation: wording toward the light / Marsha Dianne Harrison
–New York; Washington, D.C./Baltimore; Bern; Frankfurt am Main;
Berlin; Brussels; Vienna; Oxford: Lang.
(Counterpoints; Vol. 185)
ISBN 0-8204-5274-2

Cover design by Lisa Dillon

The paper in this book meets the guidelines for permanence and durability
of the Committee on Production Guidelines for Book Longevity
of the Council of Library Resources.

© 2002 Peter Lang Publishing, Inc., New York

Printed in the United States of America

This book is dedicated to the newest four chapters of my life story: Shelby Anne Smith, Wyatt Henry Smith, Torrey Jeanne Smith, and Trey Henry Harrison. It is through them I am able to see sustaining evidence that we, as human beings, continue to write and rewrite our lives and that it is through the precious life of a child that one can come closest to true peace and understanding.

Contents

Foreword by Thomas E. Barone ⤙ ix

Acknowledgments ⤙ xiii

Introduction ⤙ 1

ONE
At The River's Edge ⤙ 3
The Writer's Story

TWO
Writing and Being ⤙ 10
A Conversation with G. Lynn Nelson

THREE
Stories as Research ⤙ 28
Three Case Studies

FOUR
Interpretation of Storied Lives ⤙ 63
Fitting the Pieces Together

FIVE
Evolution and Exploration ⤙ 78
The Conceptual Journey of Narrative Based Evaluation

SIX
When You Hold a Crystal to the Light ⤙ 89
The Educative Implications of Narrative Based Evaluation

SEVEN
Musings ⤙ 102

Afterword ⤙ 107

Bibliography ⤙ 109

Foreword

Those who pay attention to developments in the social sciences and humanities are familiar with a turn toward narrative in those fields. But despite its rise to prominence in those areas of scholarship, narrative storytelling still plays a rather insignificant role in the field of educational evaluation. Through this book, Marsha Harrison contributes to the slowly growing literature in the area.

Harrison's work provides phenomenological accounts of the deeply personal experiences of students who participated in a university-based writing course. Her work offers what most traditional forms of educational evaluation—especially course evaluation—cannot. Through her intensive research, she is able to provide for readers intimate glimpses of the manner in which the lives of three students were changed, perhaps permanently, by the course and its instructor.

Readers should be aware of what to expect, and what not to expect, as they delve into this study. No balanced accounting of strengths and weaknesses of the course or its instructor is to be found herein. Harrison's intentions do not include a provision of stories that give equal weight to the pluses and minuses of qualities in the course. Instead, the author, describing herself as a "passionate participant," is persistent in her determination to illustrate the positive attributes of a course in which she was involved as both a student and as a researcher.

How can one justify such a collection of narrative accounts apparently skewed toward the affirmative? From my perspective, such an approach is acceptable only because of the shift in epistemological positions that accompanies Harrison's move into what she has labeled *Narrative Based Evaluation*. I will explain.

The traditional goal of much educational evaluation is the achievement of a degree of certainty in one's own findings. This attainment of certainty is, it seems to me, an appropriate goal when final, or summative, decisions are to be made about an educational program, course, or personnel. But such is not the intention of the author of this book. Indeed, it would be a mistake if this book were to be used for the purpose of making summative judgments about the people or programs that are characterized within it. For that purpose, a different set of premises, principles, and procedures than those found herein would need to be called into play. The more traditional methods of social sciences would need to be employed. For example, a larger number of participants—indeed, a group of randomly selected former students of the course—would need to be involved in the evaluation process.

But *Narrative Based Evaluation* represents a move away from the epistemology of certainty that is often identified with modernist social science, to a postmodernist view that no single, final meaning is to be privileged over another. In this way of thinking, all judgments made about phenomena within an evaluation text are done so within fields of power, history, and culture. Since no human being acts outside of those fields, final truths will not be forthcoming from an all-knowing evaluator or author. Indeed, the attitude of the postmodern reader must remain one of suspicion about the ultimate truth of what is contained within any text. It must be one of determination to regard the text as providing only one possible view of people and events.

The job of the postmodern author is to persuade the reader to relax this attitude. But the author does so not for the purpose of tricking the reader into accepting the text she offers as a kind of final verdict on that which has been evaluated. Rather, the author attempts to lure the reader into rethinking educational possibilities. The postmodernist narrative text is, therefore, not summative, but heuristic in its intentions. Harrison is, I believe, implicitly asking readers to wonder about the potential impact of writing courses in other places that may be similar to the one portrayed here, courses that are played out under analogous (but never identical) sets of conditions.

If that is her purpose, then it is up to each reader of the book to decide whether she has achieved it. For indeed, postmodernists would agree that reader response theorists observe that each act of reading is shaped in part by that which the reader brings to the process. That is, meaning is negotiated between reader and text within each transactional event of reading. So when it comes to *Narrative Based Evaluation: Wording Toward the Light,* I can only vouch for what it meant to me. I can report that, from my perspective, Harrison has succeeded in her heuristic intentions. How so?

Harrison has engendered empathy, enabling me to "walk in the shoes" of three former students of the course she discusses. The author accomplishes this by allowing these former students to tell their stories of change that came about as a result of their time in the course.

(The text is also autobiographical insofar as the story of Harrison's contact with the course and its teacher is also portrayed.) These stories emerge through Harrison's collection and editing of information in an interview process, and through the autobiographical writings (journal entries, narratives, and poetry) of the three students.

The carefully observed detail and vivid imagery that shine through in this chapter of the book create three distinct life journeys, enticing this reader into a set of alternative ways of being in the world. The life worlds that are portrayed are plausible; they seem real. The "tellers" may even believe that their worlds are somehow "true," but in my view, the presence of absolute or even phenomenological truth is less important than my, one reader's, acceptance of their possibility. The worlds of Marcus, Clara, and Maia are each in their own way, conceivable; they are compelling, and I am lured into them.

Once there, however, I am forced to no longer think about the worlds I have entered. For now they perform the function that good literary art performs. They demand something of me. The worlds are saturated with values, redolent with meanings of what constitutes good education and good writing. They demand that I inspect my own values regarding these same phenomena. In so doing, they sometimes perplex me, raise questions that I had not anticipated, even cause me to abandon my habitual ways of thinking about writing, and the teaching of writing, in favor of fresher ones.

Harrison also wants to prompt thinking about the relevance of narrative and life stories for the field of educational evaluation. This effort is also seen as part of a journey. In fact, two journeys seem to intersect within this book—the collective journey of members of the field of educational evaluation and the personal conceptual journey of her own as she entered into that field through the engagement in her work. Indeed, those of us who identify ourselves as educational evaluators have, as mentioned above, displayed reticence in accepting the usefulness of life stories for achieving legitimate goals of the evaluation enterprise. Our collective journey has, however, been marked by various turns that could have earlier been identified in the larger fields of the humanities and social studies. These included turns that could be identified as interpretive, literary, and finally, narrative. These turns accompanied acceptance of the more heuristic goals of evaluation that Harrison prizes.

Harrison traces many of these turns in this book as she became acquainted with them on her own personal journey. She is respectful of the leaders of the field who came before her. Michael Scriven, Robert

Stake, Egon Guba, Yvonna Lincoln, and Elliot Eisner are identified as being among the trailblazers in the collective journey of which she has become a part. Other influences from the field of narrative—for example, Donald Polkinghorne, Jean Clandinin, and Michael Connelly—are then blended into the mix. But at the end of the trail we find Harrison's own contribution as she incorporates many of the ideas and inclinations of these pioneers. As we come to participate vicariously in her personal and intellectual journey, we are prompted to reexamine our own locations on the trail of educational evaluation. As a result, some of us will move a bit further down this trail. This was certainly my own experience as I read this thought-provoking and lyrically written book.

Tom Barone

Acknowledgments

There are many people who have played important roles in the creation of this book. This has not been a solitary work, but rather one touched by many lives, ideas, and experiences. I have received so much support and encouragement along the way and I am honored by all the individuals who have helped contribute to my work.

First I would like to thank Tom Barone, who has been such a good colleague, mentor, and friend. His work in narrative research has influenced me greatly and I continually look to him for advice and guidance as I word my way toward the light.

I would like to thank Lynn Nelson and Nelson Haggerson for their continued support of this project and its message. They never tired of reading draft after draft of the initial manuscript and I relied on their sound judgment and experience with storied lives. Special thanks to Lynn Nelson for planting the idea of this text in my head and heart.

A heartfelt thanks goes out to Ivan LaCore, Ronda Woinowsky, Renee Goldtooth, and Katherine Griffith for allowing me the privilege of sharing parts of their lives with you.

I am indebted to Peter Lang Publishing for inviting me to write this book and to Bernadette Alfaro for her help with production matters. Also here, I would like to thank Margaret Carr for her invaluable help in the creation of this book.

And to my family, my parents, my children, and especially my husband Bob, for patience, and understanding, and love beyond measure. I have been richly blessed.

Introduction

$\backsim$

The sounds of storytelling are everywhere today. Narratives of many kinds are being opened and explored. Journal keeping goes on apace on all levels of learning; people write autobiographies, shape family histories, become authors of their own lives.
                                              —*Maxine Greene, 1991, p. ix*

My purpose in writing this book is to present the notion that the active use of narrative storytelling in school curriculum can have dramatic effects and rewards on many levels. When interwoven into school curriculum storytelling, or personal narrative, can have the effect of helping students, teachers, and even program and curriculum designers reach a new awareness of the power each of us holds as we put pencil to paper. The idea of narrative storytelling is the foundation upon which this book was conceived and written. During the research involved for this work, I crafted the idea of *Narrative Based Evaluation* as the conceptual underpinnings of my theory that stories are evocative, defining, and cathartic.

The reader of this book will travel the conceptual journey of *Narrative Based Evaluation* from its inception, join in a conversation with G. Lynn Nelson, a leader in the field of narrative storytelling, and hear evidence of its worth to the educational community from fellow travelers who venture down the river of our collective writing and being.

In the pages that follow, we explore the power and promise of narrative storytelling. Therefore, let me begin this journey by telling my own story.

ONE

At the River's Edge

The Writer's Story

∾

As I sit at my computer plotting the direction and substance of this work, my mind wanders back through time, back to the black and white days of my mind's camera to the genesis of my passion for stories. And I wonder when it was that I first believed in the power and magic of words.

I was a very young girl when the first storyteller entered my life. He was as thin as a reed—the equivalent of Mayberry's *Barney Fife*—always sitting hunched forward in his straight-backed living room chair, elbows resting on his bony crossed knees, hand-rolled cigarette resting between his worn knuckles. To the world, or at least our small corner of it, he was William Harvel Smith; soldier, surveyor, miner, and cowboy. To me, he was simply "my grandfather."

Some of my earliest recollections of my grandfather include my two younger sisters and me sitting cross-legged on the floor in front of him listening to story after story of his colorful life. With each embellishment of events, sparks, ashes, and loose tobacco would dance through the air and add spectacle to the enchanting recital. Stories spawned stories as his fluid memory recounted "the way things used to be" in the days before television, before telephones, before indoor plumbing. The richness of the telling drew me wide-eyed into his adventurous former selves, and I often silently cast myself as mythical figures in some imaginary playbill—the ingenue indifferent to gender or sort.

The stories my grandfather wove into the intricate fabric of his life did much more than simply entertain three young girls before supper on a Sunday afternoon. His tales took root in the fertile soil of my imagination and were nourished to vigor by the honesty and magic of the telling. I believe these early recollections of the day-to-day living of an Arizona pioneer helped shape and define the person, student, teacher, researcher, and writer I have become. Embedded in this notion, the storied lives of my family have always provided sustenance and safety for a spirit sometimes dashed by the discordant musings of reality.

On some level, my passion for the language of story led me to choose a career in education. As an English teacher for some 23 years, I have enjoyed great opportunities to explore the potency and promise of people writing their own lives.

These experiences have helped strengthen my resolve to inform and reform entrenched ways of thinking about education. Many of my concerns are interwoven, each thread of the cloth dependent on the others to create the pattern of the whole. Over the years I have become increasingly aware of changes in classroom behaviors, attitudes, expectations, and performance. Apathy toward schooling acts much like a virus, infecting all elements of education and rendering the success we seek limited and ineffectual. Neither students, nor parents, nor teachers are immune from the decline in moral character, ethical behavior, and/or spiritual decay.

It concerns me that with all our focus on standards and technology, with every innovative teaching strategy that is thrust upon teachers, and even with all the declarations of "war on poverty—drugs—crime," our society is still facing staggering numbers of children who leave our educational system unable to cope effectively with the tasks of growing up. We appear to be evolving from a community of caring to something approaching indifference and complacency. So I asked myself several questions: "What factors are contributing to this state?" "What might make a difference in the way we conduct educational practices?" and "How can we attempt to turn back the tides of alienation, neglect, apathy, and hopelessness?"

Most of us in educational arenas are constantly searching for things that "work" in our particular disciplines. I am concerned that we participate, often begrudgingly, in innovative departures from standard curriculum in feeble attempts to get at the heart of some current crisis in education. These departures usually focus on getting students motivated and more effectively involved in their own learning processes. We put our trust in curriculum designers who are often far removed from the authenticity of teaching and who are all too often driven by political agendas. We become seduced by the simplicity of repetition and practice offered by textbooks and at the same time complain that we have lost the passion for teaching that once drew us into the classroom.

I find that I am at a place in my educational and academic journey where my goals are to seek some resolution to these queries and attempt to reconceptualize current educational constructs. If we are, as the literature suggests, "storytelling creatures" (Hopkins, 1994, p. xvi), should we not, as educators, seek pedagogical structures that allow the opportunity to tell them? Should we not ask ourselves, What can we do to encourage deeper self-discovery and understanding? Isn't there more we can do to help foster peace in classrooms and communities?

I suggest that we look at a concept as old as the history of humankind itself to help rekindle the sparks that feed the fires of learning. Writing and telling our lives through stories seems rather like going back to the future, back to a more simplistic and uncomplicated method of coming to know ourselves and others. And if this is true, could the reciprocal effects of storytelling bring us all a little closer to our ultimate goal of sustained peace in our world?

From my perspective, the view of the world from my window, the simplicity of storytelling once encouraged in school curriculum has been replaced by complex programs designed by detached educational visionaries. Programs that are themselves detached from real teaching and learning. It would seem to me that revisiting the simple notion of writing our own lives continues to be a solid foundation on which to build a sound curriculum.

During my years of teaching middle school English, I decided to pursue my love of learning by working toward a master's degree. One component of my program of study was the course *Writing and Being*, ENG 494. I became a student in this class in the fall of 1988. It was then that I first became acquainted with the notions of narrative storytelling and the seeds of purpose for this book were planted. During this time I was becoming increasingly concerned about the students in my own school environment. Like them, I was struggling with a prescribed curricular diet that offered little beyond repetitious practice in correct grammar and syntax. I was becoming increasingly aware of the forces of alienation and emotional stagnation that made me question educational directives and my own effectiveness as a teacher.

As the course *Writing and Being* progressed through the semester, I had many opportunities to witness the effects of students writing and sharing the stories of their lives. I remember wondering if these concepts would help my own students in their academic, social, and emotional growth. Gradually I began to use the same lessons taught in ENG 494 with my eighth graders. I prepared my lessons with opportunities for personal storytelling through a variety of narrative genres and dialogue. As the slow process continued, I began to witness subtle transformations in attitudes, interest in learning, and general mood of the class as a community. The concepts seemed so obvious—encourage students to write their own stories (lives); provide a nonthreatening environment where sharing becomes a natural component of writing; value reflection of lived experiences as an integral element in the writing process; and conspire with students to explore ways to offset the dangerous qualities of isolation, indifference, and boredom.

Throughout my master's and doctoral work, I aligned my energies and thinking toward one goal—to that of studying the notion of storytelling as the foundational underpinnings of a sound writing curriculum. I continue to think about my grandfather and believe that stories like his and so many others have helped me to arrive at the realization that we are all storytellers, that our stories help define us as human beings, and that our stories can help us learn about ourselves and others.

In this book I have presented a study of a writing curriculum that is based on narrative storytelling and its subsequent impact on three class participants. The substance of my personal research focuses on the exploration and evaluation of a course in narrative based curriculum, *Writing and Being* (ENG 494), an undergraduate level English class offered at Arizona State University. I conducted a study to evaluate its words, work, and worth through occasions of reflection and interpretation. The book is presented in two parts: a study of the class, followed by the life histories of three respondents.

The study of the class contains an evaluative overview of the narrative course *Writing and Being*. This course is an example of a relatively new direction in education—that of employing story as curriculum, reflection, interpretation, and evaluation.

> Because the narrative process yields history, literature, and myth, and because it is central to the development of social and personal identity (culture and self)—because it is thematic (emplotted) experience—it has inescapably to do with education and learning. (Hopkins, 1994, p. 127)

Writing and Being was designed to help students explore the relationship between language/writing and the human psyche; to develop personal (journal) writing as a tool for self-understanding, growth, and learning; and to experience personal writing as an integral step in the process of producing effective public writing. The course brings together recent insights from linguistics, psychology, psychotherapy, physics, brain research, and writing/composition. It is designed to be a helpful and meaningful course for teachers, aspiring writers, and those who want to explore writing as a tool for personal growth. In this study I have focused on the curriculum, activities, attitudes, atmosphere, and instruction relative to its content and claims.

Joseph Schwab (1969, cited by Kemmis & McTaggart, 1981, pp. 91–92) wrote of four commonplaces in education as basic categories for understanding an educational situation. In this study, I kept the four commonplaces of education in mind as tools for analysis and evaluation. They were teachers, students, subject matter, and milieu. In general terms, Schwab suggested that any educational situation could be understood in terms of the interaction among these four commonplaces.

Of the four commonplaces, the notion of *milieu* is the least clearly defined. Schwab (1969, cited by Kemmis & McTaggart, 1981) stated milieu was context: "The milieu is the context of teaching and learning, creating certain kinds of opportunities and potential for education and imposing certain constraints and limitations upon it" (p. 92). I believe the milieu to be vastly important to an educational situation when conducting a program evaluation.

Dr. G. Lynn Nelson's book, *Writing and Being: Taking Back Our Lives Through the Power of Language,* is also part of the milieu. His book is based on the philosophy of the class. I looked to it as both a resource and reference for evaluation during the course of the study.

The second part of the book reflects the life histories of my three respondents. Each one had prior experience in the class *Writing and Being.* I asked each of the respondents to tell his or her story regarding the impact and influence of the class. Also included are pieces of their writing as a means of illuminating dimensions of their life histories. This writing became an interpretive text expressed by the respondents and used for educative, aesthetic, and critical consideration.

The life histories of the three respondents are presented in narrative form. Each respondent tells his or her own story, referencing ENG 494 as it contributed to any transformation or change in his or her personal or professional life, and offers personal narratives for reflection, interpretation, and evaluation. I used the concept of *writer response,* a term I coined which suggests that there is some provocative relationship between the writer and his story and that there is some possibility of change (transformation) in a person as a result of writing and sharing his personal narratives.

At the onset of this book I find it necessary to establish myself as a believer in the incredible and mysterious power of words. My own experience and practice as a writer is foundational to my assumption that stories can help us define and redefine meaning in our lives. With-erell and Noddings (1991) observed:

> Stories and narrative, whether personal or fictional, provide meaning and be-longing in our lives. They attach us to others and to our own histories by pro-viding a tapestry rich with threads of time, place, character, and even ques-tions about what we might do with our lives. The story fabric offers us images, myths, and metaphors that are morally resonant and contribute both to our knowing and our being known. (p. 2)

I believe that permission to "talk" about writing and its potential to change lives should be granted only to those who believe that

> without a story, we perish. Stories define our lives; they teach us what is pos-sible and good, help set our goals and limits, offer us role models, and explain mysteries. Without stories—myths and legends, folktales and sacred texts, romances and comedies and tragedies—our lives would be formless. (Farwell, 1988, cited by Witherell & Noddings, 1991, p. 97)

I believe in the power and usefulness of narrative storytelling as an educational tool and that this tool can offer new insights into the way we think about schooling and educational reform. Connelly and Clan-dinin (cited by Denzin & Lincoln, 1994) suggested that the recon-structed stories of people's lives are a fundamental educational tool: "People live stories, and in the telling of them reaffirm them, modify them, and create new ones. Stories educate the self and others, includ-ing the young and those, such as researchers, who are new to their com-munities" (p. 131). Along the same lines, Hopkins (1994) wrote:

> The world we live in suggests a need for a principled pedagogical structure for attending to the lives of students, a pedagogy that releases the energies of young people to master their environment and to learn through mastering their environment. (p. 2)

My personal beliefs are influenced by teachers, colleagues, mentors, and practitioners directly related to the increased attention being given to narrative and storytelling. Further, I embrace the philosophy and works of Maxine Greene (1991), who stated, "The stories we hear and the stories we tell shape the meaning and texture of our lives at every stage" (p. 1); and Jerome Bruner (cited by Witherell & Noddings, 1991), who stated, "The creative use of story and dialogue lends power to edu-cational and therapeutic experiences because of their capacity to expand our horizons of understanding and provide rich contextual information about human actors, intentions, and experiences" (p. 79). My communications with Jean Clandinin, who believes that personal narratives help us make meaning of our lives, have encouraged and "inspirited" my desire to do this work.

The writings of Tom Barone affirm my belief that the explorations into a storied life is legitimate research. From Nelson Haggerson I have learned that even simple poetry can continue to heal the spirit and make the heart *dance with joy* (Haggerson, 1971). I have explored the thinking of Catherine Riessman, Vivian Gussin Paley, Susan Sontag, Linda Hogan, Nell Noddings, Carol Witherell, Julie Cruikshank, and Jeffrey Wilhelm—writers whose beliefs about storytelling helped to inspire this work. And perhaps the greatest lessons I have learned about the power of language came from Lynn Nelson (1994), who believes that by telling our stories "we can heal ourselves" (p. 105).

Writing and Being

A Conversation with G. Lynn Nelson

⌒

Writing becomes an act of compassion toward life, the life we so often refuse to see because if we look too closely or feel too deeply, there may be no end to our suffering. But words empower us, move us beyond our suffering, and set us free. This is the sorcery of literature. We are healed by our stories.
—*Terry Tempest Williams, 1994, p. 57*

This chapter includes my experiences in ENG 494, conversations with Lynn Nelson regarding his narrative course, and some examples of his writing explorations.

Entering the River

It was a sultry September evening in 1988 when I first began the journey that would one day bring me to this work. Like any event that significantly affects a life, I remember that evening with uncommon clarity. Twenty or so people began finding a place to sit at tables arranged in horseshoe fashion. Flute music, barely audible from a tape deck, beckoned silence from students filing into the room. The room was carpeted, walled with bookshelves, and offered noninstitutional comfort of couches and easy chairs. Two lamps, adding warmth and welcome, lit the corners of the room. It occurred to me that this was unlike any classroom I had ever seen at the university. It was neither institutional nor cold, but rather pleasant and inviting—almost homelike.

Initially, I remember being somewhat suspect of the soft spoken professor who would teach the course and his ideas that seemed to depart dramatically from my previous experiences in academia. His language did not approach the terminology to which I had become accustomed in other scholarly arenas. Instead, he spoke of entering the river of writing through our feelings, dialoguing with the center of ourselves, and freeing the writer within. He said he believed in the power of our words and that we should reclaim our language and use it as a tool for self-understanding, healing, and growth. I was to find that any preconceived expectations and assumptions I had regarding the practice and purpose of writing would melt away, allowing a simple concept to emerge—that of writing my life stories.

The instructor's name is Dr. G. Lynn Nelson. He is a teacher of English at Arizona State University and the creator of ENG 494, *Writing and Being*. Dr. Nelson is also the director of the Greater Phoenix Area Writing Project, a part of the National Writing Project, and founder and director of Native Images, both a class and an outreach organization for Native American students. He has published numerous articles on teaching, writing, and the human spirit, including a book published in 1994 entitled *Writing and Being: Taking Back Our Lives Through the Power of Language*. This book surveys the curriculum, focus, and content of the English course by the same name.

Before further exploration of the course *Writing and Being*, I feel it is appropriate to quote a passage from Dr. Nelson's (1994) book:

> So, I tell you at the beginning of this book what I tell my students at the beginning of my writing classes: Here is what I hope you will get from this class (book). Ten years from now, I hope you will be sitting up some night at midnight under the light at the kitchen table—writing. Not because you have a paper due the next day or because someone has given you an "assignment"—but because you are hurting or grieving or confused, or because you need to let go of some anger. Whatever the reason you will be sitting at that table writing because you are a writer. My wish is for you to be a lifelong writer. My hope is that writing will be a tool—an emotional, intellectual, and spiritual tool—to help you survive and grow and find meaning and purpose and peace in your life. (p. 12)

This course, *Writing and Being*, was created to help students explore the relationship between language/writing and the human psyche. While most courses are concerned with the end product of the writing process—a piece of public writing (usually a critical essay or research report of some nature)—this course is different. This course focuses more on the beginning of the writing process that lies deep within us—the stories of our lives. It is as much about our feelings and our hearts and our spirituality as it is about our intellect. It has more to do with discovery and mystery and creativity than with paragraphs and semicolons. The journey into the river of writing the stories of our lives begins in the heart of the writer. For some this is not a comfortable place; it is too private or vulnerable—too risky to expose to the light. Nelson feels this course requires a different kind of commitment than other writing classes. He believes one must enter with soft eyes and a beginner's mind, things not easily given, for we have been trained to hide our feelings and protect them from harsh examination.

Entering the river then becomes a metaphor for our exploration of this unique writing course. My brief observation guides us into the stream:

> It is October 29, 1997, at about 6:45 in the evening. Class begins with quiet journal writing. A cassette tape sprinkles a piano concerto into the room and it is accompanied only by the scratchy sound of pens rushing thoughts to paper. After a few minutes the group gets up from its chairs. Thank-you notes are passed for the gifts from the previous meeting. These are small notes related to the stories (gifts) read and received. It seems very much like a ritual—students and teacher equally glad to give as to receive. And then there is another long quiet. More time for reading the notes and recognizing that personal words have touched someone on some level. Quiet reflection—like people opening gifts. Small treasures—word treasures. Affirmation. The work matters. The students are sitting in a circle. The teacher is among them. All are here to learn from one another. The teacher asks if there is any unfinished business that needs attending to. A student who wasn't in class the last time reads a piece about her grandfather. Class has begun. The journey has begun.

The name of the writing course, and subsequently the book (Nelson, 1994), has always been curious to me. At first glance at the university class schedule, students might too hastily dismiss it from consideration, perhaps not understanding what it has to offer. The following dialogue between Lynn Nelson and myself reveals what this writing course has to offer:

HARRISON: Lynn, tell me why you chose to call the course *Writing and Being.* What part does the "being" play in the process of writing personal narrative?

NELSON: *Writing and Being,* well, it took me a while to get around to that over the years, but the further that I have gotten into the process, the real process of writing, the real process of language, which is much more than we're usually led to in traditional writing and composition classes, the more that I discovered that when you are working on a real piece of writing, it's coming from within you, it can't help but change your being. So the two are inseparable.

HARRISON: This thinking does seem to depart from traditional notions about the way we learn and the process of coming to understand ourselves.

NELSON: Yes. When you are talking about traditional orthodox composition courses, of course, this seems rather absurd. Writing might affect our left brain, our narrow left brain understanding a bit, but we don't usually think of it as changing our being, changing our character, changing our way of looking at the world. And yet when we do this kind of writing, that inevitably happens—to one degree or another. Hence, the title of the course, *Writing and Being*.

HARRISON: I seem to be hearing you say that we need to rethink the way most of us have learned about the process of writing and, indeed, what the purpose of the process actually is.

NELSON: Yes, I believe so. I think that the purposes of the class *Writing and Being* are primarily to help people unlearn some of the narrow ways they've been taught to look at writing and thus at the world, and to enter the river of the power of writing and being. I suppose the overriding purpose of the course is really to help people experience—you can't lecture on that—you have to enter the river and experience it and discover that power so that they can use it for the rest of their lives. They can use it to help them deal with things that are going to happen to them in their lives through the process of telling their stories. And the design of the class has evolved to accommodate these purposes.

HARRISON: Let's talk about the design of the course. As mentioned in the syllabus, the course is designed to help students explore the relationship between language and writing and the human psyche. Is there a curricular principle upon which this design is focused?

NELSON: The foundational underpinnings of *Writing and Being* have to do with the notion of narrative storytelling. Storytelling is at the heart of the purpose, design, and curriculum of *Writing and Being*. Recently I wrote a piece called "A Writing Curriculum," which I believe speaks to the grand design of the course. It may seem rather simplistic and somewhat contrary to conventional curricular design but it seems to work for our purposes.

A Writing Curriculum

Tell me a story—a small story, a true story (or as true as you can tell it)—a story from your life. Tell me of a time when you were hurt—or afraid—or tell me of a time when you lost something—your keys, your heart, your mind, your mother or father, your way in the world—or tell me about a small joy you had today. Tell me a story—and your telling it will change you—and your telling it to me will change me—and such stories will move us both a little closer to the light. Tell me a story—and then tell me another—and I will tell you mine—and we will sit in a circle and listen carefully to each other. And then we will write thank-you notes to each other for the gifts given in these stories. And then we will do it again, anew. And we will continue doing this until everything begins to become properly precious, until we stop killing each other and destroying the Earth, until we care for it all so much that we ache, until we and the world are changed.   (Nelson, 2000, p. 12)

The guiding concept upon which this course has evolved is narrative storytelling. The format of its design began with what Lynn Nelson called the "real writing process," which begins in the heart of the writer during personal journal work, then emerges into published work to be shared with the community of writers. Nelson explained this evolution in the following dialogue:

NELSON: So we begin with a journal. I have them get a journal if they don't already have one. We talk a lot about personal writing. We do a lot of personal writing. We explore ways to use the journal as a daily kind of working place, a healing place. We spend a lot of time on personal writing, then move things out of personal writing into public writing. The course is set up so that I lead them into explorations in their journals, private personal explorations.

HARRISON: When the assignments are completed, the class meets to share stories in what is called a Feather Circle. I remember my first time in the circle. It was a bit scary—a bit uncomfortable knowing that I was about to share very personal and maybe even very painful remembrances of my life. When the feather was passed to me for the first time I remember thinking that I would embarrass myself for surely my writing wouldn't be as good as the others. I would feel inadequate. But that was not the point. The point was that I had written a piece of my life—a piece of my history. It was honest and from my heart. And that was the only requirement.

In my own experience I was a bit apprehensive at first, and there are no demands on that. There is no need to share anything you don't want to share. But almost always what happens is that people are wary at first, then the next week they come together in the Feather Circle to share stories aloud and share copies. It's always an important part of the whole process.

NELSON: I want to back up and talk about the Feather Circle idea just a bit. The *Feather Circle* has been given to me by my Native American students and friends. In the Feather Circle, there is only one rule; and that is when the feather comes to you, when you hold the feather in your hand, it is your turn to speak or to share. You must speak or share from your heart. That simple rule I have discovered produces powerful writing, powerful language. It produces language with much greater power than the narrow left-brained kind of writing, speaking, use of language that we are taught to do.

Inevitably when stories are shared in the Feather Circle, when they are read from the heart, people begin listening from the heart. There is no element of encounter group or anything like that in the Feather Circle. All we do is to listen to each other. And that simple idea also brings a whole powerful element to this, because so often in the dominant culture today, words are so cheap and most of them are manipulative words, what I call "I-it" words, words to get us to buy something. And then we become sort of immune to language, it rolls off us.

But when we come to the Feather Circle, it is a different sort of language. It is almost a ceremony. We don't have to judge anything or solve anyone's problems. We just have to listen. As Sheldon Kopp says, "Along the way as we tell our stories, there must be another there to listen." It doesn't say, "There must be another there to grade it." It doesn't say, "There must be another there to analyze it or solve it for us." So we have with language, with words, and with people, with "I and thou" in words, we have the power for great feeling and great change.

Another significant element of the writing process as Nelson viewed it is the act of writing thank-you notes for the gifts received during the Feather Circle. As I asked him to explore the concept of this practice, I was reminded of some notes I received when I took *Writing and Being* some 10 years before. I remember thinking when this assignment was first introduced that it was a little peculiar—writing thank-you notes for the gifts of personal stories.

Considering this to be a part of my inquiry, I decided to search them out. To my delight I discovered that I still had most of them, dusty and tattered though they were. Sitting at my desk, I began pouring over the comments sent by fellow students for the stories I had written so long ago. One thank-you note was for a piece called "Herculean Journey," a word photo about my son's illness. One for "The Apron" that told of the apron my grandmother always wore when she made apple pies, the one I wear now when I make them. And one for a piece called "Rosebud," a very short poem about mentoring whose words echoed a piece called "The Yellow Rose." Memories buried for over 10 years were beckoned awake—nudged to life by small slips of paper. As my mind drifted, a pause of reflection caught me wondering why I had kept the notes all these years. Probably for the same reason I save old letters and cards and family pictures. They are treasures from the past, from some chapter in the story that is my life. Nelson explained the meaning of the thank-you notes within the writing process in the following dialogue:

NELSON: Traditionally, and this was the way I was taught to teach writing, you have someone write something, usually something they don't care very much about to begin with. When they finish writing the piece, they give a copy to you, to no one else but you. You take it home, mark it up, tell them all the things they did wrong. You give it back to them with a grade on it. They throw it away and we start all over again. But this is a whole different thing. This is starting to discover the power of your words, not only in the Feather Circle, not only to help yourself and heal yourself, but you also start to get notes back from other people saying, "This touched me, this helped me," and then you start to feel the power of that process, both within yourself and to help other people as well.

HARRISON: Something that really surprised me when I took *Writing and Being* was that you participated in every phase of the writing process right along with the class. In your book you say that "knowing the river by entering it is different from standing on the bank and analyzing it." This seemed like such a simple concept and yet one that isn't used to any great extent in traditional classroom situations.

NELSON: The teacher cannot stand on the bank and say, "Go in there, it will be good for you." The only way for this to work is that I must be in the river too; I must be doing this; I must be sharing in the Feather Circle; I must be finding my own way in my own life; I must speak into a journal; I must be vulnerable; I must be willing to take risks. And this shows the way, not only in our being, but in our writing. Because writing is risk taking, writing is uncertainty, it is a struggle. So the teacher must be in the river with the students. The teacher must be a fellow swimmer in the river.

As I experienced the writing course, I began to try out some of the notions with my own middle school students and discovered that it added a whole new dimension to the community of the classroom. It is the same idea as seeing your teacher in the grocery story or at a ball game. My students began to see me as a fellow learner and they could recognize that I had insecurities and fears that were often similar to their own. They could participate in my life on a larger scale and identify experiences that were familiar to theirs.

As I mentioned earlier, Lynn Nelson offers guided explorations for journal writing and suggestions for public writing. At this point, clarity on the difference between *explorations* and *assignments* is a must. Assignments are more generic in nature, whereby the energy and thinking that goes into them are more focused on what the teacher wants rather than the personal experience and needs of the writer. Explorations are not assignments. Instead, they are opportunities for us to "peel the onion" of our lives, allowing exposure to the layers, allowing us to probe beneath the surface of our consciousness to places that might hide pain.

According to Lynn Nelson, people need to be guided into exploring these things with their writing but they do not necessarily need limitations. Nelson believes that these explorations lead students into doing the work that must be done in order to bring about changes in our writing and our being. He says that because these explorations are open-ended and adaptable, and because we are always changing, they can be done over and over again; and stories that evolve from them will continue to help us find a deeper understanding of ourselves and others.

Nelson emphasizes that at the heart of the work on our writing and being is the way we use our words to show rather than to tell. He calls this "writing real" or "words made flesh."

Explorations

I chose three explorations that are offered in the course *Writing and Being* to present here (Explorations 4, 7, and 9). I also included personal narratives by Lynn Nelson and myself to further represent the design and purpose of the explorations. This, then, becomes the real work of the course—theory into practice. This is where the process becomes real.

The following exploration is given to the class early in the semester after a discussion on memories of childhood. The writings reflected in the explorations tend to progress from childhood to the present.

Exploration #4   *Writing and Being*

AN AUTOBIOGRAPHICAL POEM

For this piece of public writing, you just share a collection of little bits and pieces of your life, like a cigar box full of souvenirs and mementos. As you are doing your "Time-Line" and "Memory Map," thousands of memories come flooding back. For this autobiographical poem, you just take a handful of them and sprinkle them throughout.

The stock of most poetry is imagery—word pictures. Think of this writing as just some picture-moments of your life. I sometimes give my students the following rules. Use them as you want; but as your poem begins to take off, let it become what it wants or needs to become:

1. Begin with something about your birth.
2. End with something about your Now.
3. In between, include lots of moments, memories, images, little pictures, of your childhood, your life.
4. Do not use any fuzzy words—no abstractions or generalizations. Let the picture you share be made only of sensory things.

The following are examples of Nelson's responses to this exploration:

BECAUSE HIS BONES REMEMBERED
by Lynn Nelson

He came from a meditation so deep and far away
only the cells in his bones remembered—
remembered slow dancing among stars and planets.
But then there was sperm and egg and
he was called back again into time,
curled like a little Buddha in Leah's womb
growing in the ocean of her simple love.

His people gave him no songs, no dances, no rituals,
no connections with the earth or the stars
from whence he came. His people were loud and grasping.
They wanted him to be happy with trinkets and toys.

But he could not—because his bones remembered.
So he was sad, always feeling like an outcast.

And because his bones remembered,
he prayed a simple awkward prayer over his first kill,
a young pheasant in the Nebraska summer cornfield;
and he secretly cried for Lorna with her face
like clawed clay, who had seizures,
who fell against the cook stove and did her
lonely dance against the fire, whose heart burst
and who was the first of his classmates to die;

and something always yearned
within him when he watched the sky grow dark
behind the windmill on the hill and the stars
whispered to his bones . . .

Only much later in his life,
in a sweat lodge in the womb of
mother earth, with the drum beating
and the old man chanting, did he begin
at last to feel at home.

ABOUT ONE OF MY LIVES
by Lynn Nelson

I was born naked in Nebraska
at the still point, the turning point,
the winter solstice.
I grew up on the farm—the windmill
on the hill stood watch over my days.
In my youth, I stepped in lots of cowshit.
Clarice Dodd sat in front of me
in the third grade. I fell in love with
her pigtails. I once saw limbs and boards
and pieces of machinery fall from the sky
after a tornado passed miles away.
The smell of geraniums will forever
remind me of my grandmother.
I have heard, after a summer rain,
the air so full of frogs' cries
I could hardly breathe. My father never hugged me,
but when I was twelve, he gave me a new-born calf
still wet from birth. I named her Queenie.
Once in June it rained for five days,
and the river came crashing to our front door
in the middle of the night.
Sometimes back then on summer nights, the stars
came down so close I could almost walk among them.
Life was a great mystery to me then—and still.

The following is a response I once made to the same exploration.

CINNAMON TEA
by Marsha Harrison

All things were right on that
summer's afternoon as we
sat quietly talking and regiving
the treasures of the previous day.
Somehow we had found ourselves
sequestered behind the large glass
windows of that sleepy little coffee house
in Durango

where reflecting sunlight
danced silently with dust and memories.
Like children tired of play
we became still, allowing only our minds
to move.
The rush of the trip
easily gave way to repose.
We sat for hours sipping cinnamon tea
from tall mugs frosted icy from the freezer,
shared the magic of Colorado, and
found delicious comfort in just being together.
We remembered Box Canyon Falls and
how frightened I was at the noise and confinement there.
I thanked you again for the milk bottle
that you had discovered in a cluttered
antique shop in Ouray.
It advertised a dairy in Walnut Grove, Minnesota—a place
familiar because of Laura Ingalls Wilder.
And I wondered how long it had waited there,
waited for us to pass by,
waited for your eye to catch it.
The tea seemed endless like the beauty and wonder
of that rocky mountain wilderness.
We sat in the stillness and worshipped alone in that
busy little cafe.
It was a time of gentle peace
and we drank of the sacrament
cinnamon tea.

The next exploration comes later in the semester. It involves looking back at our lives and finding positive things for the work of healing.

Exploration #6   *Writing and Being*

GIFTS WE ARE GIVEN:
MEMORIES THAT SUSTAIN US

Much of our work on our own history focuses upon healing wounds and exorcising monsters from our past. But we also find gifts of sustenance—moments and memories that sustain us. Memories of home and roots. Memories of the land, of special places and special times that we can go back to in our minds. Memories of little lessons learned. Remembered acts of courage or caring by others that light our way today. Precious images of people we care for and model ourselves after. Special moments of insight or understanding. Little epiphanies lost in our consciousness, waiting for us to claim their sustenance.

IN YOUR JOURNAL

As you work on your Time-Line and Map Memories, as you look back and within, many gifts and sustaining memories and images from your life emerge. Take some further time to look back over your life, and especially into your childhood, for such moments (a memory of your father's tear-stained face as you lay in a hospital bed; a moment of oneness with nature from some lost time; your hiding place among the whispering leaves of the cottonwood tree; an act of unconditional love given as a gift to you; whatever). Bring them to the surface and collect and explore them in your journal. Look carefully for images, incidents, and memories that are within you, that are meaningful to you, that perhaps have been sustaining you from beneath the surface of your consciousness (without your knowing that you knew). Begin to see and feel their power within you.

TOWARD PUBLIC WRITING

For public writing, begin moving some of these images and memories into public form of some kind to share with others. Start with just one such image from your past that sustains you and helps you in some way in your life now. Work with it until it begins to blossom into an effective sharing.

As always this a good chance to work on showing rather than telling. Let the readers feel this sustenance for themselves from the power and groundedness of your words.

Here, Lynn's response relates to a lesson learned.

FIRST KILL

by Lynn Nelson

I remember my first gun when I was thirteen—a
second-hand 410 gauge shotgun, the cherry wood stock
varnished to
a soft luster, the steel barrel dark with power;

I remember seeing the flock of young pheasants brace their
wings and drop into the cornfield below the house;

I remember clutching the gun at my side, breathing hard,
crawling through the dense rows of corn, watching for
movement somewhere up ahead;

I remember how I held my breath and squeezed the
trigger, how the gunshot exploded the stillness of the
autumn day as I fired into the rustling grass;

I remember the sound of wings all around me bursting-
rising up and out of the cornfield and into the sky;

And I remember running, gasping to those wings that beat
and beat upon the pink grass but would not, could not, ever
rise again.

My interpretation of this exploration focuses on memories of my
mother's life.

GIFTS . . . YOUR PIN CURLED HAIR
AND RED, RED LIPS
by Marsha Harrison

The most important gifts I remember
    receiving while growing up
            didn't cost money
            didn't come from a store
            didn't even really last very long
                except in my heart
the times were as fleeting as the frames
    in a kaleidoscope
            pieces to a puzzle—who I am
            patches on a quilt—what I love
I remember lunches
    of bacon sandwiches and Delaware Punch
    and how the evaporative cooler
    made everything feel sticky

while it tried to rescue us from Arizona summers
I remember you standing ankle deep
    in muddy irrigation water
    hanging clothes out to dry
            because you thought the sun made them smell so good
            and what did it matter if it made them stiff too
I remember Easter Sundays standing
    framed by yellow roses and red brick
            you beside our grandmother and behind three little girls
                boasting Kodak smiles and matching dresses
I remember the way you looked
    on the banks of the Verde River
            dishing out cold fried chicken and melty chocolate cake
    you in your white sleeveless shirt and blue peddle pushers
            your pin-curled hair and red, red lips
I remember trips to the beach
    and trips to the mountains
    and trips through your old worn picture albums
I remember paper dolls and ponytails
    and going to the movies after church
    and your amazing patience
            when I helped you in the kitchen
I remember watching you
    make school clothes
    and doll clothes and lunches for dad
I remember you telling stories
    of our family
    of a legacy rich in history
            people borne of hardened cowboys and soldiers and
    sailors and genteel ladies who tended the home
I remember the struggles and fears
    that sometimes took you far away
    sometimes when you thought
            no one could see
But most of all I remember how safe I felt having you near
    knowing you loved me—us
    knowing the softness of your hands
            your heart—your soul.

The third exploration I looked at usually takes place late in the semester when we are looking at our lives and values. It takes us to a

special place—a sacred place. It can be a place we remember from our childhood or a place that is special now.

Exploration #9   *Writing and Being*

DESERT LUMINARY

In the western sky you hang heavy like a mother carrying a child. Silently you consume my thoughts and inspirit my heart. White Against the jet of night. You take my voice and the need to use it away. I am washed in gossamer beams . . . washed in the light. . . . blessed by the light. . . .

by Marsha Harrison

IN YOUR JOURNAL

Go back in your mind and heart and look for special places you had as a child and special places that you have now. Remember places where you felt safe, places where you went to hide when times got tough, places where you could be alone. Remember what it was like there, how it felt being there, what you did there. Then pick one—the one that calls you the deepest, the one that you would like to go back to now in your writing and remembering. Focus on that one. Write it at the top of a page in your journal. Write for ten minutes putting down whatever comes to your mind and heart about that place. Remember smells and sights and sounds there. Remember what you did there and how it helped you.

FOR PUBLIC WRITING

Then for public writing next week share with us something that comes from this exploring, from this writing and seeing and being.
    Lynn writes on being on the Platte River in Nebraska.

CONFLUENCE OF WONDER
by Lynn Nelson

Eddie plays his flute, and I drift back through time to sacred space, back to early spring, back to the banks of the Platte River, back to the coming of the cranes . . .

    For thousands of years, the Platte River has made its journey from west to east across the heart of Turtle Island. It begins quietly in small springs and melting snow on the east side of the Continental Divide in the Rocky Mountains, meanders down past Denver, and then makes its way across the sprawling central plains of the continent toward the Missouri River that forms the eastern boundary of Nebraska.

Also for eons, since long before the coming of humans, each spring the Sandhill Cranes—those tall, gray mystical birds—have made their long journey from their winter homes in Texas and Mexico to their summer nesting grounds in northern Canada, the Arctic, and even Siberia. In February in the South, something in the bones of these huge birds whispers that it is time to go. On their great six-foot wingspans, they rise out of the fields and reeds of their winter foragings, gather in flocks of hundreds, and begin their trek to the far north. From all over the south, in their patterned lines and V's, they wing their way toward their northern homes.

So here are these two "streams"—one of the miracle of rain and melting snow and rising ground water flowing west to east—one of the mythical, great, wondrous birds flowing south to north. And for a few weeks within a few miles in the heart of Nebraska in the heart of the continent, these two miraculous streams converge.

I have been there. I have been there as the cranes come each spring in March, a half million of them, to these few miles on the Platte River. They come to forage and rest for a few weeks before they continue their ancient journey to the north. I have been there as these two streams converge. I have been present at the confluence of wonder. I have stood on the banks of the Platte River at sundown as the great cranes returned by the thousands from the cornfields, as they circled and filled the darkening sky with their wings, as they filled the evening air with their ancient, eerie cries, as they circled and settled onto the sandbars for the night. I have been there; and I have been touched by a sacredness beyond any mere church.

And I believe this: As long as this confluence of wonder continues, we humans may hope to survive. And I know this: When it is gone, we are all gone with it. So listen to Eddie's flute and pray with me—pray for the Platte and for the cranes and for the earth and for us.

My response to this exploration invites the reader to share a quiet memory of the mountains.

MISTED MORNING

by Marsha Harrison

Blanketed delicately
    in a silent mist
    timber cloaked mountains sleep
    while trying to avoid
    the intrusion of daybreak
gossamer remnants
    of yesterday's storm
    draw back into the hills
    shrouding life
    precious life
    fragile life
    for another day
it is so still
    so quiet
    like a pause between breathing
all sounds banished
the peacefulness of the moment
wants to last
but as the first light
    slices through the blackness
    and as the coffee
    boils seductively on the fire
I know it can't
so with closed eyes
    and my voice a whisper
    I offer a distant *thank you*
for the gift.

This, then, is what entering the river of our writing and being is all about. We are led to explore the times of our lives—to tell the stories of our lives. And in the doing of this work, what Lynn Nelson calls "the real writing process," which begins in the heart, we seek to come to a place, through our words, where we can forgive ourselves and understand ourselves and help ourselves heal the wounds of heart and spirit.

THREE

Stories as Research

Three Case Studies

⌒

Our lives are made of story: stories handed down from our parents, stories we have created out of our experience, stories about our loves, our work, our explorations, our joys, our disappointments, our learning—the soul's story. Creating story, we create and re-create ourselves.—Susan Wittig Albert, 1996, p. ix

It was deep into August many years ago that I found myself sitting, fully clothed, in the shallows of the Gunnison River in eastern Colorado. The late afternoon sun was losing its place in the sky but its slow gentle leaving touched the quiet pools around me with a halo of brilliance—a symphonic arrangement of rocks and water and light. I had been there for hours trying to will some ancient glint of gold to wash into my grandfather's battered old mining pan. My hands and feet numb from the icy remnants of just-melted snow. My back frozen in a stiffened crouch. Wet blue jeans strangling my folded legs. But even as the shadows grew long across the river and my time there grew measured, the smallest of nuggets refused to grace the hollow of the dented relic.

I look back on my gold-panning day in the Gunnison as a sort of dress rehearsal for this work. Initially, on that day so long ago, I remember being disappointed by my unsuccessful attempt to imitate my grandfather's ability to glean gold from the river's bed. Now I have come to realize that I took something more precious than gold from the waters that day. The work I am doing here is all about being in the river. It is not about choosing to sit safely upon the banks—afraid to get wet—afraid to be vulnerable to current—afraid to dig beneath the surface gravel in search of a nugget of understanding. Like the Gunnison or the Platte, the stories of our lives will take us on journeys rife with passages of turbulence and calm. Remembering the purposes of *Writing and Being,* we must be willing to enter the river with our writing and allow it to take us into the deep waters of self-discovery, understanding, and change.

In this chapter we look at the stories of three people who experienced ENG 494 *Writing and Being.* They tell some of their life stories and offer pieces of their writing as evidence of their journey down the river. In their stories they shared some of the rough passages of their lives with honesty and in the spirit of edification. They also shared the common belief that through the writing and telling of stories—the real writing process—people can begin to identify old wounds and set upon a course to heal them. Each story is presented in the respondent's own voice.

Marcus' Story

Marcus Brown is a Language Arts Specialist in Roswell, New Mexico. Most of his professional career has been spent teaching English, biology, and physical education at the middle school and high school levels. His favorite school assignment came in 1993 when he began teaching senior high students at Rough Rock Community School in Chinle, Arizona. Marcus is an accomplished writer, athlete, and educator. I met Marcus in 1988 when we were both in the *Writing and Being* class for the first time.

I ended up taking the *Writing and Being* course because so many of my colleagues recommended it. I remember asking them what it was all about but they would just stumble a bit saying, "You know, you really can't say, you just have to be there to find out on your own because it's a discovery." Indeed, it was a discovery. I found out quite a lot about myself as a result of this course.

Saying this class is wonderful doesn't really say anything. That's just a generic word people use too much. But on the other hand, it was wonderful because it took me on a journey deep within myself so that I could recognize, for the first time, old pain and anger that consumed much of my life. It was an awakening of sorts, a realization that my heart had scars on it caused primarily by my father, and one way to heal those scars was to write the stories of my life.

This discovery process starts in the journal. This is where the real writing begins. Here we are given permission to bring forth the hurt from our subconscious mind and lay it on the table. The amazing thing here is that I began writing about things I had kept hidden for years. I had a whole bunch of stuff buried inside me that I didn't even know about—stuff that was really hurting me—maybe even killing me. I think one of the strong points of the class was the idea of sitting in silence. I don't know if we used the word meditation, but we would sit there for two or three minutes and listen to our own breathing. That, I had never done before. I thought this was great because I could imagine myself blending with my own breathing, so that I became my own breathing. It was a centering experience. From this quiet time we would go to our journal writing.

In the early years of my education, I remember my teachers asking me to write from my own resources, but they didn't teach me how to do that. After all, you can't just say, "Well, you're a writer, sit down and begin." This was something different. Lynn taught us how to tap the stories within us. It wasn't so much a direct tap but rather an exploration of the times of our lives. It's all about discovering things inside yourself and if you're willing to enter the river with your words, then this whole great wonderful dialogue comes out through your pen. That's the part I really love. It's like magic. I wouldn't say it always happens because a lot of us let things get in the way, but if people buy into this notion and if someone gives you permission to write, then to some degree you can begin to touch what's really going on inside.

You see, I came to this class with a lot of baggage. Tremendous baggage, and I didn't even know it. I was probably 45 years old when I took this class. That's a lot of years to hide things from myself. And when my stories started coming out through my writing, it was a shocking experience. Not always comfortable. But I came to a place when I welcomed them to come out. I always felt better. I've heard people say, "Well, I just can't write like that because it's just too painful." And I respect that. But for me, I had to do this because of the way I was raised. Odd bits and pieces of my life began to come together and it was hurtful—but a good kind of hurt—a cleansing hurt.

Let me share with you one of my first poems. This is about my father and it is called "Being a Child in My Parents' Home."

BEING A CHILD IN MY PARENTS' HOME

Crossing the train trestle into the night,
steel beams girded the bridge like a cage.
The heavy end of vibration weight
pulling a string of cars.

Around the curve, onto the bridge
the shifting Cycloptic light,
sound of the whistle, blasting like heat,
dust drifting up from the track.

Engine splitting the night like an arrow,
tiny man driving the beast.

I hugged a steel girder,
finger tips digging a layer of soot,
diesel smoke pulling my face.

Wheel bearings smashing industrial glass,
a black tie orchestra clanging a floodgate
into the night . . .
and gone.

Now, I know this may sound like a bunch of craziness all mixed up. And if it does, well this is how I felt being around my father. This is a metaphorical journey of me being with my father. Being around him was like trying to cross a railroad bridge at night when you can't see very well, and this train is bearing down on you, and you've got nowhere to go. And hear the "sound of the whistle, blasting like heat," he had a loud voice, he would yell. That would scare me. And so it goes on in this way.

My father was a drug addict and he would go into these rages. But I really didn't know that as a child. I didn't know about it until I started writing things down about him. I am a child in this piece. I'm trying to touch it as I remember it, and I remember him as being a really mean guy that I was afraid of. This touches me because these images are how I remember my father. So it's good for me to get this written down. In all the craziness that's going on here I have learned something. Look at the last lines, "Wheel bearings smashing industrial glass, a black tie orchestra clanging a floodgate into the night . . . and gone." I learned something here—

I learned that I lived with a crazy man as a kid. In my own mind, the best part of this poem is that I can make images that capture the feeling of how it was as a child, even though this whole poem is a metaphor, because my father is not really a train. But the train stands for him. There is no love in this poem, just fear.

"Being a Child in My Parents' Home" opened the door for me to take a look at what was going on in my life. It actually became the door for future writings. After a great deal of work in my journal, I was able to further explore my relationship with my father in a second poem. In this piece ("Saw My Father in a Dream") I am an older person, looking back, seeing my father and myself from a child's point of view.

SAW MY FATHER IN A DREAM

I wanted to tell him how I close my eyes to see
when sliding down the salty surf.
He wouldn't listen, and I turned away
as he lectured me.

When I was a boy, we had reading practice
so I would do well in school,
become a doctor too.

I remember once, his oak paneled study,
he wore a starched white shirt and tie
and slapped me on the head.
  "Read the damn book."

I started to cry.
Tears twisted letters on the page,
I stumbled over the words.

  "Do you want to grow up to be a ditch digger,
  work with a shovel all your life?" he growled.
  "Why do I have a kid like you?"

To get even, I scrambled letters through my tears.
Doctor became *Dotcor*—Bubble became *Babble*,
a lexicon of bongo words,
a sea wall against the surf.

I'm older now, have learned
to scribble out feelings in a journal book:
    a slight turning without the tears,
    a smile,
    a changing slant of light.
Letters don't jump around so much,
words mostly stopped shaking.

And now, I wonder
what it was like for my father to have a boy:
    who didn't read well,
    would never be a doctor
    and wouldn't even try.

This poem gets at the heart at what was going on between my father and me. Or at least it comes closer. He had high expectations for me. He was a doctor himself and he wanted me to be one as well. But the thing is, he is so busy being a doctor that he never plays with me. He's never even around much. And when he was, he was mean. He didn't even find out that I couldn't read until I was in the fifth grade. So we had reading practice. So he slaps me on the head, like it says here in the poem. And he gets mad. Reading, then, became a painful thing. I hated it. I hated him. And my hatred was so huge that I purposely didn't read, just to embarrass him. I thought that having a kid who couldn't read would hurt him and that was a way to get even.

Look at the line that goes "a slight turning without the tears, a smile, a changing slant of light": that means that I now have new tools to work with. I have a journal book. My father never had a journal book. I have my own power and it's in the journal—it's in my words. After I let this settle on my mind a while, I found the need to write a third poem about my father and me. I see it as a further attempt to get rid of my anger I felt for him. Actually getting rid of the anger is a by-product. Now, here's a clue. I love the ocean—more so than most other people. So I'm at the ocean thinking about stuff, writing about stuff, watching the dolphins—and then something happens to the ocean. Here's what happens. I am beginning to see that my love for the ocean is stronger than the hatred I have for my father. These two forces meet and this is the result. This piece is called "The Dolphin."

THE DOLPHIN

Morning sunshine, sound of the surf.
I stood on the breakwater,
looked over the Pacific, several dolphins
swimming, rolling their way south.

"Come here and see me. I am Marcus," I yelled.

They paid no attention but stopped to frolic:
tail stands and flips, bumping each other in midair.

"If you're going to ignore me, I'll wait right here," I said.

I lay down by a chiseled inscription in the breakwater,
"Built in 1909," and thought,
That's when my father was born.
He and this rocky ledge, relics of yesteryear.

I hadn't seen my father for years,
a stern man when I was a boy,
hated his criticism all the time,
but resting there, my fear seemed old and far away.

I moved my fingers over the eroded inscription,
mossy and salt crusted, wondered how my father was doing.

Soon the dolphins began moving south.
One left the others, rode the underside of a wave,
then surfaced, looked its ebony eye at me.

I wanted to run into the ocean,
hug the dolphin,
be as good as could be.
But it exhaled a spray through its blowhole

turned . . . and rejoined the sea.

I began to wonder who *we* were.

   Look back to the passage that begins, "Resting there my fear
(my father) seemed old and far away," and where I talk about my
love for the ocean. It seems that these two forces, the love for the

ocean and the bad feelings for my father are brought to the same part of my consciousness. And all at once so much is going on. It occurred to me that maybe the dolphin was my father and since I wanted to hug the dolphin, well, maybe I didn't hate my father anymore. But the dolphin goes back to rejoin the sea and I have to go back to the land.

So we have this great meeting of the sea and my father and the dolphin—momentarily welcome together and then go our own way. I think that what happened because of the writing of this piece is that although I still don't like my father much—I don't hate him as much as I used to. I felt like I had a new kind of "me" going on—one without the anger that had eaten me up for most of my life. Looking back on the three pieces of writing, I see that I have made a huge transition from terrible hatred and anger, to a place of peace within myself. Or at least a place approaching peace. Not exactly forgiveness but maybe something more like an understanding.

Marcus believed that, through his writing, he had successfully re-solved some issues regarding his relationship with his father but real-ized he had never really addressed problems with his mother. In the following pages Marcus talks about those issues through his poetry and conversation.

I've written quite a lot about my father but, strangely, nothing about my mother. I couldn't figure out why. Who was my mother? There seemed to be a blank in my mind, a section that was absent from my life. I knew I was afraid of my father, but who was my mother? I tried to think about her and I tried to feel about her—as an adult and as a child. But I couldn't do it very well.

I do remember going home after I received my undergraduate degree. She had put the picture, of me graduating from college, in the local newspaper. When she did that, then I began to identify some of the old feelings I had for her. Some of the pain I used to have, started to come back, too. I tried to capture some of it in this poem. She puts my picture in the paper, and then I begin to see her. I call it "Pictures in Perspective."

PICTURES IN PERSPECTIVE

When I got my college degree,
you put my picture in the paper,
the society page, Mother.
My sister's picture too,
a degree from Columbia.

Noticeably absent from the paper,
a picture of Father
and a caption that didn't say
      Marcus A. Brown, M.D.
      addict to drugs,
      abuses his wife,
      and children.

Yet, our father's contribution
reverberates, Mother:
      Your denial through the years.
      My anger a hollow bullet.
      Sister swallowing her lies,
      still choking in her children
      long after Father is dead.

Put that in the paper, Mother.
Or did it slip your mind?

Here it seems like my mother wanted to emphasize all the superficial things. She liked to impress the neighbors with things that didn't seem to mean much, and at the same time she was hiding the fact that our father was a drug addict. She was a person of denial. In the fourth stanza, "Your denial through the years" spoke directly to me. How did her denial affect me? My anger became a "hollow bullet." But she denied everything, at least all the bad stuff in our family.

Well, writing this straightforward piece got me thinking that I had a lot of other things to work on regarding my mother. I was beginning to find out that my mother was a great deal more than the empty place in my mind and heart. This poem caused me to look at her more closely and try to find some missing pieces of the puzzle. Gradually, through my journal work, I began letting my

mother emerge into the light. I began to see who she was when I
was a child growing up in my father's house. Here is what I wrote.
And it isn't nice but—

A DEAD ELEPHANT IN OUR LIVING ROOM

"Your father and I, we love you very much," she would say,
but I heard a twisting in my heart.
Each deception supporting the previous distortion
until everything she said was covered up
like her Siamese cat scratching in its litterbox.

You were the boss, Mother.
rode your pony like a rough rider,
red wine in your saddlebags,
demons in your heart.

There wasn't time for me,
just time for . . .
        filing your fingernails
        smoking cigarettes
        admiring your reflection in the mirror.

I didn't really have a mother,
wasn't much of a son.
I was more like an Ethan Allen coffee table
she would show off to the doctors' wives,
or her purebred Siamese cat
        she was going to neuter
        if he didn't stop spraying her walls.

There was a dead elephant
in our living room, Mother.
We always stepped around it
never mentioned it,
thinking maybe it would go away.

But it stunk a little more
each year . . .

Writing this poem caused me to see that my mother was a
sneak. She kept everything that was ugly a secret. That's why I

didn't even know her. Look at the third stanza where it says, "There wasn't time for me, just time for . . ." It seemed that every time I wanted to talk to my mother, she was always filing her fingernails. She would stick her hands out at arm's length as if to say, "Stay away from me, my nails are more important to me than you are." Her image was everything to her, her cigarettes and her reflection in the mirror. Because of this poem I see that just about the only satisfaction she got in life was seeing how pretty she was in the mirror. She never got any pleasure from anything else.

I never thought about any of this until I began writing in my journal. Then things just started exploding from the pages. Memories and pain flooded back and I was able to put my finger on some things that have bothered me for years.

It does hurt to write about many of these times in my life. It hurts to see these words on a piece of paper but somehow, in the doing of this, the hurt becomes less severe, less of a threat. Because I can write about the hurt I have experienced, I begin to realize that I have choices—choices regarding which baggage I want to carry and which I want to let go. Understand that simply writing stories about my life doesn't always heal things completely but it goes a long way in that process. I still have things to work on regarding my relationship with my parents, and some of it I might never get resolved. But I have jumped into this river with my writing and intend to use it as a tool to help save myself.

All of this began for me in the *Writing and Being* class. Writing in a journal, writing the stories of my life, things that are important to me and that have a connection to me. I know a lot of the time we tend to push aside those things that cause us grief because we are too afraid of our feelings. But really we are people of the heart. And when we recognize the heart, just like when we recognize our feelings in a journal exploration, we begin to see a change in the way we treat ourselves and others in our lives. Our spirit changes. Our attitude changes.

That, for me, has made all the difference.

Clara's Story

I introduce Clara Bee in the Native way. She is of the Diné (Navajo) people. She is of the Salt Water clan, born for the Cliff Dweller People. Her maternal grandfathers are of the Towering House clan and her paternal grandfathers are of the Red Running Into the Water People. These clans identify her as a Diné woman. Clara is 28 years old. She is a senior at Arizona State University, majoring in biology and premedicine.

As a way of further introducing Clara, I include the following piece called "Female Warrior," written as a response to the Autobiographical Poem Exploration from the *Writing and Being* class.

FEMALE WARRIOR

I am from playful tumbleweeds and dusty valleys,
red mesas and blue mountains,
the place where mother was born.
In the womb of the hogan she set her feet on that corn pollen road.

Across dry rivers, a young boy felt a kiss in the winter wind,
on his chapped cheeks.
He would be the one I would call father.

Before I was born
my parents felt my spirit
present in the round, warm hogan
between laced logs and packed mud.
I lay curled in mother's womb listening to words of my grandfather.
The three of us were married.
I was born that year and set my feet on that corn pollen road
and learned where I was from.

I am from smiling ancestors,
from elders with stories of Coyote and the lizard.
I am from trailing tears on brown faces
looking back at land, sheep, and corn, taken in the name of
    assimilation.

I am from unemployed relatives.
I am from those unkept BIA roads.
I am from alcoholic brothers and sisters.
I am from their
            abuse,
             neglect,
        from poverty,
        and starvation.

I am survival.

I am sacred prayers from grandfathers and grandmothers,
from elders of the Diné and Hopi Nation,
from Barboncito and Manuelito.

I am from sacred ceremonies
from harmony of voice and drum,
from earth colored rugs
from medicine,
from the four directions.

I am from those who keep my feet on the path to become this

female warrior.

It seems like I've been going to school for too long. It has been
pretty hard at times to keep focused on what I really want to do.
Being a Navajo and a woman also puts me in a rather unique situation as far as my field of study is concerned. I come from a culture very different from what I am exposed to here at school.
Sometimes the two parts of my life seem conflicted with one another. Navajo ways and Anglo ways are very different.

Because of my major, I have been required to take many science
and math classes that will help prepare me for medical school.
The coursework is very difficult and I have to work so hard to
keep up. Sometimes I feel like I might lose my way. One course,
however, has helped me survive the struggles of being an American Indian woman living in two worlds. I found *Writing and Being*
in the fall of 1996 and since that time I have been writing stories
from my heart.

The English classes I took before coming to Arizona State were
very different from *Writing and Being*. I remember when I was a
student at Navajo Community College, I was enrolled in a creative writing class. I thought it would be fun, you know, something
interesting and different from the stress of science classes. But I
ended up not liking it. By the end of the semester, I knew that
writing wasn't for me. It wasn't personal writing. It was something far away that wasn't touching me. I decided that I wasn't a
writer—I couldn't think of myself as a writer.

Looking back on that class, I think my trouble came from not being able to identify with the assignments. There was very little of myself in them. Once, the instructor gave the class a packet of kachinas. The packet had maybe ten pages of information and images of the kachinas. She wanted us to look at them and then write about something that came to us. Now, kachinas are gods of the Hopi people. I'm a little bit Hopi but not that much. And I don't know the Hopi ways. I remember just looking at the pictures and wondering, "How does she expect me to write about this?" In the end, I didn't have anything to say. I think my paper only had three lines or so on it.

The same kind of things went on in my freshman English classes. ENG 101 and 102 were just something I had to get through. I didn't connect myself to any of the assignments and I'm not sure I took anything substantial from them. And then in 1996, I enrolled in ENG 494, *Writing and Being.*

I guess old habits are hard to break and I remember looking at Lynn Nelson and thinking, "Another *White* teacher . . . why am I taking this class? I don't want to do this." But in the first few minutes, I realized that this was going to be different from any class I had ever taken before.

Our first assignment was to buy a journal. A journal! I remember thinking that now I would have to be writing something about myself. This was kind of upsetting to me. I was learning about biology. I was learning about the sciences. I didn't have time to be pouring my guts out in a journal. I didn't have time for this emotional mentality. But I was to buy a journal—so I did.

It was the second night of class and we all had to show that we had bought a journal. He (Lynn Nelson) asked us to hold them up so everyone could see them and then he did a curious thing. He set a kitchen timer for ten minutes, turned a tape on in his cassette recorder, and said to "just write." And, I didn't know what to write about. After what seemed like an eternity, I scribbled the first line of my journal entry—"This is my new journal." I had nothing else to write about. So I began thinking, "What 'should' I write about?" That was it. Something clicked somewhere for me and I started putting down all the things that were going on inside me at that moment. All at once it felt good to be in that room.

Things changed dramatically after that. I was correct in thinking that this would be different from my other English or writing classes. The teacher wanted us to write about ourselves and to tell our stories—that's all he wanted us to do. That's when I thought, "Wow, somebody actually wants to hear our stories. And we're here at ASU, so how often are you going to hear that?" I think it was very important for him to say that he wanted me to write my stories—especially if you're an Indian, it's really important.

One of the first things he wanted from us was a story of our home when we were young. I remember writing about being on the reservation. Some of my most favorite memories are of my life as a young girl in Chinle.

My mother is a dental assistant and I used to spend a lot of my free time at the dental clinic playing with toothbrushes. Those were sort of my toys, something to keep me busy and quiet while I sat by my mother while she worked. Sometimes she would also have to work at the hospital so I was always in the company of doctors and nurses and dentists. Before long they were saying that I should become a dentist or a doctor when I grew up. I didn't really pay them much mind but I was actually comfortable being around doctors and hospitals. It was a very natural place for me to be. I suppose my interest in medicine began there, there and the fact that my grandfather was a medicine man.

It wasn't too long before I got to ASU that my grandfather died. He was the medicine man, he was my grandfather, he was everything to me. And he was dead. I was so full of grief and so far away from home that I couldn't do anything. I thought of his gifts of healing people and his sweet gentle ways with me, his granddaughter. Anyway, the full impact of losing my grandfather hit me when I took Writing and Being. The teacher wanted us to write our lives, so I began writing the stories of my life on the reservation with my grandfather, the medicine man. One of my stories turned into a piece called *Shi'chei bi'jish*, or "My Grandfather's Medicine Bag."

Shi'chei bi'jish
MY GRANDFATHER'S MEDICINE BAG

Sitting on a metal folding chair you hold the ends of the white yarn and make funny faces at me while Grandma stands behind you folding your hair into a *tsiiyeel.*

I wash your paisley scarf in a silver metal basin with cold water and generic detergent while you take the green metal trunk with tarnished silver corners down from its place.

Inside the trunk, your *jish*, a medicine bag, lays quietly amongst jars of colored sand and herbs wrapped in red cloth with tiny yellow flowers, indistinguishable now, but remembered from years before.

Your aged hands disappear into one side of the old pouch and reappear holding small bundles of buckskin stretched around *good* medicine.

On the concrete floor the sun makes a rectangular shape where you, me, and the iron stove sit forming a circle before the doorway. The smell of fresh cedar and sage surround us as you pull bigger bundles of herbs from your pouch. Male and female prayer sticks and the bundles are packed carefully inside a smaller buckskin.

"You probably need these too." I hold up the bundle of black and white feathers, "pa," toward the door to show you that I know what they are for.

The tops of your moccasins face each other as you pack them in the pouch. Before putting the gourd made of turtle shell inside, you shake it and sing a song about the blessing of grandchildren.

Tonight your songs will be prayer songs to the sacred beings. Legs crossed beneath you, left arm on your leg, gourd on your right. Rhythm kept as you instruct sons to sprinkle corn pollen to the four directions inside the hogan.

Loose brown trousers, a good choice for medicine men, red plaid shirt over white, you stand in the sun. The scarf tied around your head, knot in back, receding white hairline seen from the top.

Brown Pendleton blanket, *jish*, rolled inside the blanket and two cans of warm Shasta cola under your left arm you walk to your blue Chevrolet horse.

"Shi'kaad shitsoi": I am leaving now my grandchild.

I will be just like you grandfather, a great medicine woman, I will walk with you always within me, a song in my heart, and one day a medicine bag to call my own.

I think this piece, about my grandfather, was a good place for me to start writing my stories. It made me realize that I had a whole lot going on inside me. I was living far away from my home going to a huge university. I was a Navajo and a woman trying to make my way in a predominately Anglo-male-dominated academic area, and my beloved grandfather had just passed away. Writing this piece got me thinking about what it meant to be a Navajo—about my culture and traditions and ceremonies. It made me really think about what I wanted to do with my life—and even where I wanted to settle.

This poem came from an exploration called "The Word Photo." The idea is to picture in your mind's camera a place or event or even a person who is very special to you. Because I was struggling with my grandfather's death, naturally he came to mind to write about. The way I pictured him with my words in this poem is the way I want to remember him. Not the way he was at the end, in a hospital dying of cancer, but setting out to perform his healing medicine or to conduct a ceremony. I tried to picture him as clearly as possible and that really helped me, because in a way, I got my grandfather back.

Much of what I write about has to do with the struggles of the people in my native culture. Writing these stories took me on a journey into my past and made me open my eyes to some things that caused me great pain. I have found that through the writing of these struggles I gain a sense of peace and come to a place of healing in my heart.

I think it's hard to be a spiritual, traditional person now in 1998. It's hard being here in this culture trying to cope with the demands of this school and this society, and trying to maintain my Native heritage at the same time. I found a way to help me survive the personal struggles in my life—and that way is by writing the stories of my life. My grandfathers and their grandfathers and the generations before didn't write their stories. They didn't know how to write. Instead they relied on the Oral Tradition. Unfortunately many of the rich stories of the Native People died with my grand-fathers. Lost to me are the times of their lives—their fears, their accomplishments, their joys. I believe that in searching for their stories—I will find my own.

So in the meantime, I am here on this big university campus, learning how to become a medicine woman in the "White Man's" world and trying to balance the old ways with the new. Writing my story along this journey seems to help it all make sense. I have found that there is great power in my words. Like a blessing cere-mony, they offer "good medicine" to the struggles of my heart. Let me leave you with a prayer I offered to the spirit of an animal whose life touched mine in one of my biology classes.

LITTLE ONES

Sat in the belly of the hogan
      heat from the iron stove
Legs outstretched, palms upward, eyes closed . . .

Remembering dissection of my frogs, my turtles, and the
      beautiful white rabbit with pink eyes.
Remembering the warmth of their blood
      and the miraculous movements of their hearts.

Thank you little ones for your life and for the knowledge.
You have honored me with your life.

My little ones,
      do you affect my spirit,
      do you hate me?

Hear this prayer my grandfather sings,
My legs outstretched, palms upward, eyes closed . . .

      I will be just like you grandfather,
      a great medicine woman,
    I will walk with you always within me,
      a song in my heart
    and one day a medicine bag
      to call my own.

Maia's Story

Maia Huntley is a 26-year-old schoolteacher from Seattle, Washington. She has a degree in Spanish and has taught ESL and dual language classes in Phoenix. During high school, Maia traveled to Australia as part of the Rotary Youth Exchange and in 1994 she received the Rotary Foundation Ambassadorial Scholarship to study in Granada, Spain. In 1997 Maia spent five weeks in the summer institute of The Greater Phoenix Area Writing Project on the campus of Arizona State University. At the time of this writing, Maia has just returned from Guatemala.

Much of Maia's story seems to focus on her identity—who she was, who she is now, and who she might become. She reflects on her childhood and those people whose lives touched hers in some way. She looks at her professional life as a teacher—a new teacher—and openly tells of her insecurities, frustrations, and confusion. She wonders about her future—the Maia she might become. Through all of this she writes. The struggles with her emerging selves serve as rapids as she swims in the river of her writing and being.

One of the first things we did in *Writing and Being* was to write an "Initial Position Paper." Let me see if I can make you understand the concept here. On the first day of class the teacher asks you to go home and write freely for an hour or two about some feelings you have going on inside of yourself. This is strictly private writing—no one will read it except yourself at the end of the semester. It's an exercise in reflection and discovery.

The teacher gives us ideas to prompt our thinking but is careful to say these are not questions to be answered. Instead they are only things we may want to wonder about in our writing. Things like: How are you feeling about yourself right now? What things are you struggling with? What things feel good, positive, energy giving? What feels negative, energy draining? What makes you smile? What makes you cry? What feels like it needs or wants to change? We also had to give some thought to our writing experiences—how we were taught to write, did we keep a personal journal, and what memories did we have that were associated with school and writing.

I want to include some of that initial paper because I believe it is a fitting prelude for my story.

Excerpt from "Initial Position Paper" (September 1997)

I like the idea of doing this paper, although I'm a bit skeptical that I'll be able to sit and write for two hours. How I feel about my teaching is so wrapped up in every other aspect of my life right now. I don't know if I can honestly or fairly answer how I am feeling right now. Overall, I would have to say I'm bitter about teaching because it has consumed my life. I'm not really a person anymore. I'm just a teacher. I've pretty much lost my sense of self, and instead I measure my days by how well or bad my teaching experience went. The frustrating thing is that I've never tried so hard to fail. I really connected with that line in the front of Shapiro's book about Teach for America where he wrote that part of his interest in TFA was seeing how overachievers handled the frustration of inner-city schools. That's me alright—frustrated. I'm at a point where I wonder if my experience is shaped by who I am or if it's just par for the course for a novice teacher.

When I wrote this piece I was just settling into my second year of teaching. Looking back on my first year in the classroom I recognized that none of my previous training or coursework had sufficiently prepared me for the realities of teaching. I fought to just keep my head above water and most of the time I had trouble finding much satisfaction in any part of my life. Adding to the mire of frustration and anxiety that threatened to choke me was the death of my father in September of that year. So much happened in that one year. It was probably the most turbulent of my life.

So here I am with my rookie year tucked under my belt saying, "Here I come, ready or not," mostly "not" as I head back to the classroom. Something tells me I should be looking forward to new challenges and new beginnings but there are still too many ragged edges in the hem of my life and I continue to stumble about, unable to find solid footing. And the wound of my father's death is still too fresh and my heart hasn't healed much in a year's time.

The summer before I took ENG 494 *Writing and Being*, I was involved in The Greater Phoenix Area Writing Project. It was there that I first met Lynn Nelson and became acquainted with his notions regarding the writing process. During that time I became a devoted journal keeper and came to regard my personal writing as a means to deal with the tremendous emotional stress I was going through. By the time I came to *Writing and Being*, I was fairly familiar with Lynn's belief that there is great power in the stories of our lives and I was looking forward to searching deeper within myself to continue the healing process I had begun in the summer.

One thing you should know about me—I'm a perfectionist. Now this is a really huge part of who I am and it has caused some difficulty for me when it comes to writing my stories. I think a lot of people shy away from writing because they think, "If it's not just perfect, then it's not good." Usually I feel more comfortable working in my journal where there are no rules—no English teacher sitting on my shoulder. I remember struggling with my father's death and the fact that I wasn't there with him. You see, he died. And then it was over. He didn't want a funeral so there was no closure. Just like that, it was over, which, I think is bizarre. When I came to Writing and Being, I was still trying to make some sense of the issues surrounding my father but the perfectionist in me kept getting in the way. I want to share a passage from my journal that speaks to this.

JOURNAL ENTRY (9–8–97)

I am struggling as usual to write my piece for tomorrow. It's so frustrating to be of the frame of mind that whatever I write has to be perfect. I can speak and speak and not concern myself whether someone has heard me, because once the words are spoken they are lost. Writing, on the other hand, captures all my glaring imperfections. I suppose I shouldn't worry so much about what is not right, but I can't help myself. I think that is part of my frustration with athletics. How do I perform without practice? How I practice without other people seeing me? That's a Catch 22 situation. Instead of trying to solve that puzzle, I should just learn to accept my imperfections and limitations. If I did, how would that change me? I think I would be different to some degree because I would be more relaxed—maybe a little more haphazard, probably a lot more. I would record my flood of ideas and feelings instead of resorting to the never ending pages of pre-writes and lists, and spend that time preparing. I wonder if I can consider that composition time, a time during which my brain is wrestling with the words and trying to put them in just the right order. But in the effort am I sabotaging my own creativity? I have to wonder . . . and be frustrated.

I am encouraged by my choice of words in the last line here: "I have to wonder." I find that I do this "wondering" more and more as I continue my journal writing. This is a healthy place to begin. It is a safe place to begin. One of Lynn Nelson's admonitions to his students regarding the journaling phase of the writing process is that there should be no rules. It is not a place to worry about spelling and sentence structure but rather a place of personal discovery. It's a place to take out the garbage that builds up much like it does in our homes. It's a private place—a place to explore my life without any fear of judgment or criticism. I have a lot of garbage to take out.

By writing about my struggles with always "needing to be perfect" in my journal, I have been able to make some progress in telling the stories that need to be told. The discovery is that it is more important to write stories from my heart than it is to have a manuscript that is mechanically correct but devoid of depth or feeling—or healing. I think it's all about being willing to jump into that river. You shouldn't deny yourself the pleasure of the water because you don't know how to swim. I couldn't deny myself the experience of writing about my father or my teaching because the effort might fall short of perfection.

Being able to write my stories has helped me cope with some tremendous pain and frustration in my life—a lot of it coming within the last few years. I am a new teacher, I am grieving for my father, and I am struggling with the concepts of love and acceptance. I learned in *Writing and Being* that we should look at writing as a tool to help identify our pain and move toward healing the wounds life can bring our way. I believe that I have come a long way in my journey toward those ends. As part of my story, I want to share some pieces that have helped me come to a better understanding of myself and those who have affected my life.

The first one is called, "Words Unspoken." It is about my father and the first piece I wrote in Writing and Being.

WORDS UNSPOKEN

If silence were truly golden, my father would be a wealthy man. Many things have changed, but the silence still remains. Hour after hour after hour alone and we still have not exchanged a word. He lies in his bed facing his death in much the same way he lived life: half asleep with an open book slipped down by his side, talk show blasting on the radio, images from the boob tube dancing among the shadows on the wall. I steal glances at him and in those few moments when we make eye contact we have one of the many conversations that I have imagined in my mind.

I understand how difficult it is for you to speak, but just for once I want you to say how proud you are of me to my face. Tell me that you are afraid of dying because you'll never be able to teach my children to hang spoons from their noses. Tell me anything at all.

I wonder at the irony of it all. Here is a man whose life was run by addictions. He used to pour poison down his throat to hide from emotional pain and I condemned him for it; now the poison is pumped into his veins every ten minutes to kill the physical pain. He smoked because it was one of life's simpler pleasures; now he smokes because it is his only pleasure; I condemn him for it.

Don't you understand that the cancer sticks are what have made you beholden to the machines? You used to breathe life into machines, but now it is the machines that breathe life into you.

He used to be a world-traveler—it was the only thing we had in common. He worked in Poland practicing his craft and he came back with presents and photos of himself in a world where he felt at home. Sharing those photos was an excuse for him to talk. There are the ones of him with Stefan and the ones of him with that kid who tried to teach him Polish. And there are albums of him in places with people that I never knew.

Thank you for my gifts, dad. They're beautiful. You know, those photos don't have any labels and I can't remember who is who. Why didn't you call Stefan to tell him that you were sick? Who is going to call him and tell him you've died? Why didn't you tell anyone you were sick?

He doesn't look like the man in the pictures anymore. He looks like a Holocaust victim, with his distended belly, swollen feet, and hospital rags hanging from his skeleton. They're the only things that won't rub against the incisions where they put in the tubes. He won't be taking any more trips, even though he thought he would. He actually bought them presents—a Huskies sweatshirt, some Legos, blue jeans—they're all sitting in a big Tupperware container at his house. Now the only "trips" he makes are from his bed in mom's living room to the porch to have a smoke. It takes him an hour, round trip, with stops along the way to refuel with oxygen.

How the hell can you still smoke? Don't you know the oxygen could explode? How can you make it to the porch, but you don't have enough energy to make it to the next room to go to the bathroom? This is mom's house, you know. Years ago you asked her to leave yours and now here you are shitting in her living room. I don't understand you two. I never will.

He almost died once already this summer. He was living at our house at Moses Lake with my little brother and something went radically wrong. Matt called the ambulance and they took him to the emergency room. Someone at the hospital said that he didn't have any DNR papers so they had to resuscitate him. Matt says that he told them that dad wanted to be let go. In either case, they brought him back. I was in Houston at the time, learning how to "Teach for America." I'll never forget hyperventilating over the phone as my mom told me that he probably wouldn't make it through the night. Wouldn't a good daughter have been on the next plane home to spend time with her father in his dying days? "Your father would not want you to give up your life to come watch him die. He's so proud of you and how far you have gone in life; he wouldn't want you to give up your dreams for him." Turns out that the nurse that changed his morphine bag that weekend forgot to turn the pump back on. He almost died from withdrawal or pain, I'm not sure which. I hope she has to live through that terror some day.

You know, it's hard for me to talk to you now because this may be the last time that I will see you. On the other hand, I don't want to see you again because that would mean that you have endured another couple of months in this miserable condition that some people call life. I hardly see it that way. This is more death than living and it makes me incredibly sad.

I hate myself for not having the courage to break the silence, but I don't know what to say and even if I did, I don't know if the words would change anything. Words were never important to my dad. This is the hardest thing for me to accept about him. It's funny because my mother has paid thousands of dollars attending seminars to learn how to manage the gift that my father practices in his quiet, nonjudgmental way: the art of being.

You asked me once in a drunken phone conversation if you had been a good father and I said—"yes." I lied. I was convinced it was the alcohol talking and not you. Ask me again without the poison, okay? Ask me again and this is what I'll tell you: You are—My father. My silent teacher showing me what matters: Gentleness and love for all creatures without a voice—the cats and chickens and rabbits of the world. Acceptance of people regardless of their social stature, income, or appearance. Freedom can be found in poverty as in wealth. Part of unconditional love is allowing others to make their own decisions regardless of the consequences. Addictions are real, ugly beasts that choose to rear their heads at the most inopportune moments. It's never too late to bridge the gap. The words I LOVE YOU still mean something to some people.

And I do love him.

The history of "Words Unspoken" is that it comes from two journal writings. Basically this was a retrospective piece from the time that I last saw my father. It was the last time I visited my dad. I was sitting in my mom's living room and trying to get up the courage to go and talk to him, because he and I had never been close. And I couldn't do it. So I thought, "Well, I'll write him a letter in my journal." You see, I have this really crazy habit of writing letters to people when I can't work up the courage to say what I want to say in person. And I remember it was kind of funny, because usually when I write my letters I will give them to the people for whom they are intended. This time I didn't. So my father never actually heard any of this while he was alive. Of course, the conversation never took place as the title says "Words Unspoken."

The poem is actually kind of a dialogue, but it's a dialogue between my conscience and what I'm saying. So the first stanza describes my father. The second stanza is what I would say to him if I were given the opportunity. The third stanza, again flashing back to describing; the fourth, what I would say; and alternating back and forth.

As far as the process of writing this goes, it was the first thing I wrote in *Writing and Being,* so it was particularly difficult. I didn't quite know how to sit down and just write. I had a lot of reservations because, of course, I was not a writer, I was a friend of writers. I wondered how on earth I was ever going to get anything down on paper. And after hearing Lynn read his first piece about his father, I thought my first piece had to be about my father, even though it was crazy and insane to take on something that huge in my very first writing.

The first draft I did of this piece was actually very different from the final version. I selected part of my journal writing where it says, "Hours and hours and hours alone with my dad"—and I still hadn't worked up the courage to talk to him or write him a letter. So many questions began exploding in my mind at this time. If he weren't nearly dead, would I be writing him a letter? Why now—because it is expected of me? Will I feel better knowing that I at least did something? In the end, I thought that maybe it would be best if I just wrote a letter to myself so I could figure out what was so difficult about all of this.

Basically, what I ended up doing was taking this letter to myself from my journal and interspersing it with one I had written nearly a year later. The result is the dialogue you see here.

The process of writing that whole piece was obviously very painful, but it was also very healing, because it gave me a chance to get down and get out what I didn't ever get down or out when my dad was still alive. In some ways, I think it was an opportunity for me to convince myself that he was hearing what I had to say. I was really very angry with him for dying, and angry with him for not talking to me, and angry with him for being an alcoholic. I didn't know what to do with all that anger. Writing this story was a start.

I believe it is also good and healthy to share this with other people. I think that my sharing this with everyone in my class was very bonding, because then other people would share their stories about their fathers or their husbands or uncles or brothers. I remember one reaction from my writing group came from Peter who said, "After having heard your story, I decided to go home last night and call my brother who has diabetes. I haven't spoken to him in quite some time because of a family argument over something stupid. I realized that this was ridiculous, so thank you for inspiring me to say what I avoided saying up to this point."

So maybe this writing could be used almost as a kind of teaching tool—to get people to communicate their feelings no matter how difficult the circumstances might be. Some people say, "Don't wait too long or you won't have a chance to do something." I like to think that the story of my dad and me carries a lot of different "waits." It probably does for other folks too.

The second piece I have included in my story is called "Annie Jo."

ANNIE JO

She's the favorite aunt, come to save her
niece from Smalltown, USA. She's trips
to Mount Shasta and Cannon Beach and
Crater Lake. She's dining out a couple of
times per week. She's screaming (singing)
in her sleep. She's cakes and candy and
candy and cakes. She's tired. She's
church and youth group. She's the floral
shop at 6 A.M. She's irritable. She
grounded me? For not making my bed?
She's backrubs and Sunday night TV.
She's upset again. She's smiling. She's
unreasonable. She asked for it—I'm
outta here. She's "Meno"—what? She's the
Confectionery Cottage. She has leukemia.
She's in remission. She's not, she is, not,
is, not, is, not . . .

This poem is the result of some work I did in my journal as part
of the Memory Map Exploration. In class, Lynn asked us to create a
memory map and I chose to do one about my life in Portland, Ore-
gon where I lived with my aunt and uncle. In the process of trying
to do the map, I remember struggling with things to put on it. It
had been a long time since I lived in Portland and all my memories
seemed very superficial. But I could remember my aunt, so I
started writing down as many things about her as I could.

I gave a collection of my writings to my mother for Christmas
and I included "Annie Jo" in it. After she read it she said, "You
know, what you managed to do is capture the essence of my sister
in a very positive way, probably better than anyone else could." I
felt good about that, because my mother and my aunt didn't get
along too well. They weren't bosom buddies. My aunt was always
the perfect child and my mom was kind of the black sheep rebel of
the family. It was nice to be able to share my vision of what my
aunt was with my mom.

When I shared this piece with the class it was one of three small
"word photos" so I don't remember if I actually read it out loud.
People in class did read it though, because I remember getting several "thank you" notes for it. People complimented me on this

portrayal of a woman who was very important in my life and whose imminent death was heavy on my soul. In retrospect, it was really good to have written this before she died. In looking at the difference between writing this piece about my aunt before she dies and writing the piece about my dad after he died, they are completely different. One was so much more of a celebration of life, and the other was so much more of a struggle with death. I think it shows growth in my person and in how I deal with the whole process of death and dying.

The next piece I will share is called "Child Bearing Hips." One night we had a guest writer who came to class and led us on an exploration about our own conception. I thought, "Oh wow," because my conception story was not probably one that was going to be very happy. I knew that my mother had married my biological father (not the man who died in Unspoken Words) on the rebound from her divorce from her first husband. She didn't pick the best of men. He was a jerk. He was a psychopathic liar. He beat my sister. He was wanted for rape in Washington, and I knew all kinds of things about him that weren't positive. Before she knew she was pregnant with me she filed for divorce from this man. During my journal work on this exploration, I got to thinking that my mom's conception stories are incredible.

We've always had this running joke in our family about all of the women having child bearing hips, because we have very small waists and very big hips for our small frames. I decided to write a piece about my mom and about the stories that I knew about her.

CHILD BEARING HIPS

> Small frame, big hips.
> Child bearing hips
> like my mother's.
> She tells me her stories
> to keep me from bearing too soon,
> before either of us is ready.
> Her first, a baby girl conceived
> in the passion of young love.
> Her second girl, unexpected,
> conceived while under sedation.
> At last, a boy, as prophesied.
> An unfaithful husband,

an ugly divorce . . .
with a child on the way.
The doctor says she can abort,
eight months later I am born.
A woman alone with four children.
A blind date, a fling, a love child,
another marriage.
An alcoholic.
Another divorce.
Nothing about these big hips
guarantees that bearing children
will be painless.

I showed this piece to the class and when I read the first two lines, "Small frame, big hips. Child bearing hips like my mother's," everyone laughed because there is a back-handed humor in the whole thing. People were kind of shocked that I would take this in a humorous direction and then lead into something that is really tragic and sad if you know all of it. One person in the class even said, "That wasn't very nice of you."

But I think this is a true reflection of my perceptions and feelings about marriage and commitment and having kids. Even today, as I look back on this piece and even writing in my journal about my conception, I see how my mother's experiences have tainted my own experiences somewhat and influenced me in the way I choose to live my life. I think that writing this piece helped me to understand that my mother's life is not mine, and that my choices are mine, and that I can live my life not in fear of what she went through because while we might be very similar in some ways, we are not the same.

This piece was written after my first year of teaching in Phoenix, Arizona. I came to Phoenix from the Teach for America program thinking I was going to have a job teaching sixth graders in a gifted program with bilingual kids. My elation soon turned into frustration when I was told that this position no longer existed and instead, my job would be to teach recent immigrant students with interrupted schooling, which meant that they had recently come to the United States from Mexico and Guatemala. The first objective was to bring them up to grade level and then to teach them English.

So I had eight students and those eight students and I were crammed into half of an old home economics room. We had our

own little partitioned wall, but we could hear and smell everything that they did in home ec. It was a very frustrating experience; and not only because it was my first year of teaching, I didn't
know what I was supposed to be teaching. I didn't have a curriculum. I didn't have anything to go by as far as a model for my program. I didn't have any space and I didn't have any windows. I remember going to the vice principal in October and telling him
that I didn't think I could do this anymore. Somehow I did, but not
without some serious concerns on my part. I felt very defeated. I
felt like I had nothing to show for the year's work. Writing this
made me realize I did.

What I did here is to write along the same lines as the piece
about my father. Instead of my thoughts, however, I took parts of
my students' journal entries and put them alongside of my own. I
tried to get some perspective on what the year had been like for all
of us.

MAESTRA

And so my first year begins—one week for preparation, two
weeks of teaching, one week off for the funeral, another week of
teaching, and it feels like I've been doing this forever. I have
worked so hard to give these kids what they need and they are
just flat unappreciative. The most frustrating thing of all is that I
give and give and give and they don't even like me. Those little
brats. I should feel guilty as I write this but cynicism has replaced
idealism.

We missed you very much. I wanted you to come back to do the
work that you left for us and to read to us from Mrs. Frisby of
NIMH because now I don't even remember what Mrs. Frisby is
doing. Now all of the work is messed up because the other teacher
left everything unorganized and she freaked out. She lost my story
about the explorer.   *Luis*

I am sick of hearing, "I don't know what to write," at journal time.
Why do I have to put up with all their whining? Why can't they
just act like human beings instead of animals, and do what I tell
them to do? This is so frustrating. I know that the punishments
that I hand out are unfair, but I don't know what I am doing and
I'm no good at faking it.

You are a good person. You are not going to believe it, but you are like an aunt to me. That is good because my aunts live in Mexico and I don't see them very often now, but then you came. You are a good person and we all love you, Maestra, but when you get angry the guys get angry with you and then you punish them and they do not listen to you and you get angry a lot. But in any case, you are a good person.   *Lupita*

I hate this class, especially the band leader, Enrique. They need to get that little shit out of my class because I am sick of his antics. I should write an essay about how difficult it is to smile while teaching. Or better yet, how difficult it is to love the children when all they do is piss me off. Ah, the joys of making so much money—so I can do what? Spend my days yelling at children? Why must I fight them? And why can't I do it in my own language?

My Maestra is very special to me, even though sometimes we get very angry with one another and she sends me to detention, but she is special to me and when we have a problem she always helps us and gives us ideas about how we can come out ahead. That's why I will always love her very much and she will always be a special person for me. Every day I like her more and even when she looks furious with me I will always care for her.

Enrique

I ask myself why I ever thought I'd enjoy education in the first place. Sitting around a bunch of unmotivated children is not my idea of a good time. I don't understand why I should care if they don't. Take Jose for example: He showed promise, but honestly can't do anything if you don't hold his hand along the way. "I'm tired," he says. Tired? I'll show you tired. Working all day with all of you and then going home to work six hours more. That's justifiably tired. What you are is lazy.

In Mexico when I was six years old my dad always bought me clothing like pants, shoes, shirts and now that I am older my dad doesn't even buy me shoes. I buy my shoes because I work. He rarely gives me anything to eat and when he does, it isn't much because for quite some time he hasn't bought me anything. My sisters and I have been working to buy food because my father doesn't love me or my sister, only his other daughters.   *Jose*

Back from yet another field trip and all Rio did was complain. "I don't wanna go," "I don't wanna walk," "I'm hungry," "I forgot my lunch," "I don't wanna sit next to her," "I wanna go home now," "I can't decide what to buy," "The people don't understand what I'm trying to say, go buy it for me," "Why can't we take the bus home?"—and the list goes on.

Maestra, when are we going to go to the park that we went to last Wednesday to take photos and play and give food to all of the ducks and pet them and we'll get there by walking like we did last time.   *Rio*

My first year of teaching is finally over and I say "good riddance." This year had its good moments, but I have never tried so hard to fail . . . I lost my class, I lost my sense of purpose, I lost my sense of self. I work with only eight students all year long and they have nothing to show for it. I look at their test scores and I realize that I didn't teach them anything. I came into this profession believing that "one day, all children will have the opportunity to attain an excellent education." Just not with me as their teacher.

The thing that I liked best about this year was that we did many wonderful things all together and that we really enjoyed ourselves with you this year. I am very happy with you because you have taught us a lot and you have supported us a lot this year. I have never had a teacher like you. I thank you so much because you have been very good to us after battling so much with us. I hope that you like everything that I write here and also that which I did not have to write. I love you very much, Maestra.   *Dulce*

This piece was hard for me to write and when I shared it in class, I cried. It was very emotional and the pain of that year was still raw. Remember, I'm a perfectionist, so I had this sense of failure and I didn't appreciate the fact that I wasn't good at something.

This piece got a lot of attention in the months after it was written. Many people told me that this is exactly like they had felt on occasion and there was this realization that my feelings weren't so uncommon or cruel. It was just my honest account of my feelings toward my teaching situation. It also made me realize that I wasn't a complete failure after all because, on some level, I had touched my students' lives. Through their words they were able to show me the truly important thing—things that were kept hidden by the frustrations.

The last piece I'm going to share with you is called "Epitaph" and was written in November. The object was to identify the things in your life that drive you crazy and change them into something positive. I think the point I am trying to make here is that I am perceived by my friends and peers as this super efficient organized person who doesn't have a lot of feelings or emotions. This is really strange to me because throughout my life I have always been a real sap—you know, I cry, I laugh, I do things on a whim. I'm a very emotional redhead who can fly into a rage and fly into the giggles at the same time. Here in Phoenix, I don't have a lot of friends who see me as that really human person. I think I shut that part of myself down during my first year of teaching. Anyway, I wanted people to see the other side of my personality. So here it is. This is me screaming from the mountaintop saying, "Hey, I am a human, and you need to think of me as such."

EPITAPH

Her death was tragic, especially for one so young. Her body gave up in desperation, to save her soul. The elders of the village met to discuss her epitaph: "Here lies one who was . . . Intense. Responsible. Precise. Machine-like. Organized. Neat. Quick. Persistent. Earnest. Eager. Hard-working. Devoted. Enterprising. Stubborn." Her soul, eager as it was, quickly re-entered the world of the living. Her second death was equally tragic. Her body could take no more; it had lived a long, full life. The elders of the village met once again to discuss her epitaph.

Here lies one who . . .

Fed her lover pomegranates by candlelight
Told the rude woman in the supermarket to have a nice day
  and meant it
Let the hair on her arms and legs grow as long as it pleased
Watched a project fail knowing she could have saved it, but
  chose not to
Threw away her dirty clothes and bought new ones
Read a storybook each day with a small child curled up in her lap

Took a nap with her students after lunch and let one of them be
    the good fairy that woke everyone up using a magic wand
Kissed a stranger on New Year's Eve and danced with glee
    when she found out that he was her prince charming
Sat for hours on end in front of a crackling fire, sipping hot
    Russian tea and reading a new Irving novel
Rode a galloping horse into a storm
Got married in a big stone church, wearing a forest green dress
Wore her freckles with pride on a sunny Arizona day
Laughed aloud in class at her students' stupid jokes
Embraced her friends each day, as if it was the last day that
    they might see one another
Planted a garden of carnations outside the window of a bed-
    ridden redhead
Snorkeled with the sharks off the Great Barrier Reef
Bought a new pair of shoes for every day of the week
Received a compliment with gladness in her heart and a smile
    in her eyes
Lived as irresponsibly as she possibly could
And was loved for it.

I think what I'm getting at here is that I don't want to be known as someone who doesn't know how to live irresponsibly. And that's why I made this whole notion of the first soul dying and the second soul coming back and doing all of the things that I maybe wouldn't necessarily do in this lifetime, but might do in a future lifetime.

I'm not completely happy with this piece. I think it needs work, but then, I need work too. I feel like this is a collection of ideas and visions that I have for my life and things that I want to happen, all at once.

As part of the class evaluation I wrote some things that I feel are appropriate here. In part I wrote, "My day-to-day life has not really changed much since I started this class. I still face the mundane trials of my life, trying to figure out how to reconcile my simple child-like mind with my super-serious, responsible side." I think that came out in "Epitaph," where I wrote about the things I would love to be remembered for. Unfortunately, I have created a world for myself where the responsible woman rules. Because of the semester in Writing and Being, I really started to reflect on what is important to me and my happiness.

One focus for me during my time in Writing and Being has been my family and the role they play in my life. I am still not quite sure how much I want them in my life but I think I have worked hard to hold grudges against my family members for not being the people that I think they can be. I am still struggling with unconditional love and acceptance. Putting my struggles down on paper and sharing them with my class have made it easier for me to see where I need work personally.

I have changed in many ways as a result of my experiences in Writing and Being. I have chosen some really tough issues in my life to bring into the light through my stories, and can honestly say that I am at a better place because of it. I am still struggling with my teaching and trying to do whatever it is one does when a new relationship starts. I will write in my journal about these things more and maybe even find a story or two there. I'll work on this in the summer, while I'm sitting in the jungles of Guatemala.

FOUR

Interpretation of Storied Lives

Fitting the Pieces Together

∽

*All persons are puzzles until at last we find in some word or act
the key to the man, to the woman; straightaway all their past
words and actions lie in the light before us.*
—*Ralph Waldo Emerson,*
International Thesaurus of Quotations, *1970, p. 713*

The notion of change is reflected in every facet of this project. The
writer who crafts a story from the experiences of a life acts in much the
same way as a skilled stonecutter who brings forth a dazzling gem from
the shards of an ancient rock. Each seeks to hold his work up to the
light, to allow the warmth of its clarity to stir our passions, and to regard its sculpted image as a precious treasure.

Changes in a person's being can be as subtle as a leaf falling onto a
glassy pond or as explosive as a bolt of lightning ripping through a
desert sky. Storytelling—the telling of our lived experiences—can at
once suffocate us with crushing pain and breathe healing life into our
faded spirits.

Some literature tends to suggest that the complicity of writing and
sharing our stories helps us to define and understand who we are and
who we might become. With all the scholarly evidence I have found
that supports this notion, I choose the grand simplicity of Witherell
and Noddings (1991) when they write, "The stories we hear and the stories we tell shape the meaning and texture of our lives at every stage
and juncture" (p. 1).

Maia, Clara, and Marcus have each shared a portion of their lives
with us through the words and work of their stories. They have all been

impacted by their experiences in *Writing and Being*, and all have sought to heal the wounds of heart and spirit by their explorations through the writing process. All were at different places when they began their journeys and each chose a different river in which to swim. What these three students brought to the class and what they took from it now becomes the gemstone we must hold up to the light and whose reflection will measure its worth.

To begin my discussion here, I want to revisit Lynn Nelson's interpretation of the "real writing process." This review helps to attach significance to any relationships we might discover between the practice of writing personal narratives and the appearance or suggestion of change.

Once, in a conversation with Lynn Nelson, I remember him saying, "To enter the river of the writing process—and the process of our being—we must begin at the source: With our feelings." The process of learning from ourselves has its roots in the acknowledgment that we are, at our very centers, creatures guided by deeply rooted feelings and emotional baggage. This is where many of us store our fears and anger. This is where we keep our grief and pain and confusion. Many people choose to deny these feelings and prefer to keep them hidden. By not consciously recognizing the honest emotional struggles that touch our lives and make us human, we are often visited by unhealthy and even dangerous consequences.

So the journey into the river of our writing and being begins with the feelings of the heart. The process continues as we start to explore those feelings and attend to their existence. At this point we find words to identify what we are feeling in our heart. We begin to build upon these words by looking at images and dreams and memories that want to shroud our feelings in a veil of mystery. We bring them into the light and out of the darkness. These impressions become the tools that help us survive.

The next step of the process happens when we begin exploring our thoughts and images and memories through personal writing—our journal work. Nelson (1994) suggested that personal writing in our journals is the heart of all our writing (p. 37). There, our words become tools for our psychological, intellectual, and spiritual growth.

From the private work of a personal journal, new observations begin to emerge and find form and substance. This is where the stories of our lives are transformed into pieces of public writing—those involving an audience. Nelson believed (1994) that the form that the pieces take should be allowed to evolve naturally. Some pieces "want" to become a poem, or a letter, or a story, or any number of things. Keep in mind, it is the process, as opposed to the final presentation, that is truly important.

The last step in the writing process is to share your work with others, giving voice to your words. In the *Writing and Being* class this happens in the ceremony of the Feather Circle.

Now, with the whole writing process and the potential for personal transformation in mind, let us look again at the stories of Marcus, Clara, and Maia for evidence of growth in their personal, professional, and spiritual lives.

Marcus came to the class bearing the heavy burden of hatred for his father on his heart. He said that his feelings for his father had festered for years and that, to some degree, they had affected the way he conducted his life. Before coming to *Writing and Being,* Marcus had never thought to write his anger and pain in what he called a "journal book." Instead he acted out his feelings—throwing temper tantrums, intentionally trying to embarrass his parents, and refusing to learn to read. Now, he considers his personal writing and stories to be a continual journey of discovery and survival: "This class took me on a journey deep within myself so that I could recognize, for the first time, old pain and anger that consumed much of my life."

Marcus believes that the three pieces he selected for this study show a change in the way he thinks and feels about his father. He sees them as a sort of journey of recovery from the craziness of his childhood memories to a more healthy, peaceful understanding about his past that he now enjoys.

"Being a Child in My Parents' Home" is a narrative fraught with angry and violent images: "The shifting *Cycloptic* light, sound of the whistle blasting like heat, . . . I hugged a steel girder, . . . [and] wheel bearings smashing industrial glass." To Marcus, this is what it felt like being around his father. The train that is his father, in this poem, is constantly bearing down on him and he has "nowhere to go." These are the recollections of a child living in a home where fear and cruelty replaced love.

Marcus recognized that he had further work to do if he were to continue the healing process he had begun in the first piece. He stated he worked a great deal in his journal exploring his troubled relationship, trying to see his father from a different perspective, and even trying to see himself through his father's eyes. "Saw My Father in a Dream" reflects the struggles of a little boy unable to please his overbearing father, but there are other things going on here as well. Marcus says that this piece gets closer to the heart of the problems between his father and himself. He puts the effects of drinking and drug addiction aside in this piece and shows us specific instances where he and his father caused one another pain. There seems to be a somewhat softer tone to this piece—almost a reckoning with his father, absolving him of complete blame for the estrangement. He writes, "And now, I wonder what it was like for my father to have a boy who didn't read well, who would never be a doctor, and wouldn't even try."

Marcus makes another discovery that turns up in this poem. He says:

> Look at the line that goes, "slight turning without tears, a smile, a changing slant of light." That means that now I have new tools to work with. I have a journal book. My father never had a journal book.

And he wonders, "Would that have made a difference?"

By the time Marcus writes the third piece, he is well on his way down the river to a closer understanding of his father and himself. The *dolphin* bears little resemblance to the harshness and frustration situated in his first piece. Instead there is a peacefulness—an almost dreamlike quality—that surrounds the poem. In this piece, Marcus looks at his father through the eyes of a grown man who has come to terms with much of the pain in his past. Instead of seeing his father as a train "engine splitting the night like an arrow," now his father might just be a dolphin, "one [who] left the others, rode the underside of a wave, . . . surfaced [and] looked its ebony eye at me."

Marcus says that these stories have taken away much of the anger he used to carry hidden in his heart. He admits that, while he does not hate his father anymore, he still does not like him very much. And he thinks that is a much better place to be.

Marcus' two pieces about his feelings toward his mother seem to parallel the poems about his father. Initially they began as angry voices and then worked into stories edged with something approaching understanding and empathy. He writes of the whole process, "I never thought about any of this until I began writing in my journal. Then things started exploding from the pages and I was able to put my finger on some things that have bothered me for years."

I asked Marcus if he had changed in any way after being involved in *Writing and Being*. It had been over ten years and I wondered if he continued to practice any of the writing process in his daily life. Marcus says that the biggest change in his life, as a result of the class, has been the realization that instead of acting out his fears and pain in negative ways as his father did, he can write about the struggles and suffering in ways that are positive and constructive. He says he is a dedicated journal keeper and believes the practice of writing his stories (his life) and participating in writing groups in New Mexico and California continues to be a source of comfort and personal growth.

Clara brought different struggles to *Writing and Being*. She brought the cultural heritage of the Native American, the pressures of a young Navajo woman trying to live in two worlds, and the scholarly involvements of a premed student. Upon her arrival to the class, the collision of the three was taking its toll on her attitude, her health, her relationships, and her performance in school.

Initially she was skeptical of the course, fearing it would be like the writing classes she had taken before. She never felt successful in her earlier attempts at writing. She said the assignments were not connected to her life in any way; therefore, she did not learn from the process of doing them.

Clara also admits to having great difficulty adjusting to the notion of journal writing. It was such a foreign concept to her that she was stymied and unable to go much beyond, "This is my new journal." But as her pen seemed to freeze over the paper, she had an epiphany. She began thinking of the things that she should write about: her struggles with leaving the reservation, grief over the loss of her grandfather, her identity as a woman, her studies. She stated that, all at once, she had too much to say and that the words of her heart began flooding the blank pages of her new journal. She had just jumped into the river of her writing and being.

The writing process took Clara on many journeys as she worked on the explorations for the course. Many of the seeds she planted in her journal emerged into powerful stories of her family and academic life.

When Clara first came to Arizona State University she was mourning the loss of her grandfather. The shock of his death overwhelmed her, leaving her unable to function constructively on any level. One of the seeds she planted in her journal that first night of class contained images of her grandfather. Her first attempt at writing the stories of her life, "My Grandfather's Medicine Bag," is a response to an exploration called "The Word Photo." She says this exploration gave her great comfort as she worked on it because she was able to put the picture of her grandfather preparing for a ceremony into the camera of her mind where it will remain focused and never lose its sharp clarity. She leaves us with images like, "I wash your paisley scarf in a silver metal basin," "loose brown trousers," "red plaid shirt over white," "brown Pendleton blanket," and "two cans of warm Shasta cola under your left arm as you walk to your blue Chevrolet horse."

By writing this narrative—taking this word photo of her grandfather—Clara says she is now more able to focus on the richness of his life than on the heartache of his death. Her heart had healed some. Writing it also caused Clara to realize that she had other healing to do, much of it involving the ugliness of alcoholism in her native culture. The confusion of a young girl trying to understand, "Is alcohol medicine? Is this like Grandfather Peyote, taking your mind and prayers to another level, to feel the prayer, to hear the Holy Ones, to communicate the pain of an Indian man?" Hard questions to answer. Harder questions to ask.

Clara brings some hard issues into the light through her stories. She says that being given the opportunity to write about them and share them with others has allowed her to attend to her ailing spirit. Clarissa Pinkola Estes (cited by Albert, 1996, p. 4) tells us "Stories are medicine." This metaphor is sustained by Clara when she says, "I have found that there is great power in my words. Like a blessing ceremony, they offer 'good medicine' to the struggles of my heart."

For *Maia*, the first year of teaching was very difficult for many reasons. She was thrust into a situation she was not prepared to handle. The physical layout of the classroom met neither her needs nor those of her students. Her expectations for herself and her students were unrealistic. She was overwhelmed by paperwork. She felt alienated from her family, and her father had just passed away. She writes, "Being able to write and share my stories has helped me cope with some tremendous pain and frustration."

By her own admission, Maia had become very bitter about teaching, relating that it had consumed her whole life and made her a negative person. She said she had lost her sense of self and could no longer identify a clear purpose in what she was doing. When she writes in her "Initial Position Paper" of these frustrations, she seems to be wrestling with a myriad of conflicting emotions. As her story unfolds, we find that the anguish over her professional life has been complicated by the death of her father. Maia is in a bad way.

By the time Maia came to *Writing and Being* she was already a devoted journal keeper and letter writer. We learn that she writes letters to people telling them with her heart the words she cannot seem to say with her voice. Though she is somewhat a novice at journal writing, she has been writing letters for years. So she comes to the class with the knowledge that she brings with her a powerful ally—her stories.

"Words Unspoken" seems to be a combination of letter writing and journal work, something she calls a dialogue between her "conscience and conscious." It is a piece she has to write to help heal the wound in her heart caused by her father's death. But it is much more than that. It is an attempt to have a conversation with her father and tell him all the things she has kept silent for most of her life. She is troubled by her father's miserable condition, much of which she attributes to his smoking and drinking. She wonders why he cannot bring himself to tell her he is proud of her. She is not ready to let him go—even though the alternative means extended suffering.

Maia remembers thinking she had taken on too much in choosing this piece so early in the course. She wanted to create a meaningful statement to her father—some powerful piece of writing that would let him know her innermost thoughts about their relationship. Her desires were lofty but the perfectionist side of her wanted to control the direction and substance of her words. Rather than risk imperfection in a narrative to her father, Maia chose to write a letter to herself asking why she was having so much difficulty expressing her thoughts. The dialogue presented in "Words Unspoken" is the result.

Maia read this piece in the Feather Circle one evening in class and the harsh realities of her father's cancer were made public. The hot tears and choking voice of the fatherless child would not keep Maia from telling her story. She believes that writing our words is only part of the journey—that there is an extra dimension to the whole process of growth when we share them with others.

"Maestra" was born out of the frustration Maia felt as a novice teacher. This piece started as grumblings in her journal—musings and complaints about the glamorous job of being an educator. Maia wanted the piece to reflect the failures she assumed were hers, but the work ended up taking her in a completely different direction. This was a surprise. A redemption of sorts. With the help of her writing group, Maia was able to craft a piece of writing that has allowed her to recognize and applaud her successes instead of focusing on her failures.

Maia believes she is in a better place emotionally and spiritually because of her participation in *Writing and Being*. She says she has come to regard her stories as instruments of self-discovery and enlightenment as she goes about her daily life.

Common Themes

All the storytellers included here agree that some amount of pain was involved in the explorations through the writing process. It seems to be the monster nipping at the writer's heels as he or she runs toward the river. Sometimes it is a secret buried deep in a heart, or a ragged scar on a suffering soul, or an anger that wants to rule a mind. It must also be said that all three participants have worked through some of the pain in their lives through this process. I think "process" is an important concept to note here because this is work that never really gets finished—it simply moves us further down the river in the journey of our "coming to know."

Through my interviews and conversations with the study participants, and the actual construction of this project, I discovered several common themes. They seem to weave the three stories together and join the storytellers into a kind of community of learners.

One theme surrounded the social issues of drug addiction and alcoholism. They touched each life represented here. Marcus says his father was a doctor but a drug addict as well. He was not aware of this as a child; he only suffered the results of the addiction. He remembers his father being a really mean man who scared him. His father was the train crashing into the night who slapped his son because he could not read—who abused his family with neglect and anger. His mother "rode her pony like a rough rider, red wine in her saddlebags, demons in her heart."

Clara writes of the pain and suffering her family endured related to the abuse of alcohol. She is haunted by this systemic problem and how it has affected her culture. She tells us how the sacred ceremonies of the American Indian are being compromised by passing the whiskey bottle instead of the prayer stick. She said that, "Christians drink wine as the blood of Jesus but her people drink the peyote medicine of cheap wine like it is tea."

Maia shares her father's death with us. By the time we meet him his body is wasted from the lingering effects of smoking and drinking. He is left to suffer the cruel indignities of cancer. For many years he had poured poison down his throat and smoked because they were life's simple pleasures. Maia tells us that addictions are "real beasts that choose to rear their ugly heads at the most inopportune moments."

Death and the shadow of suffering emerged as another theme in these case studies. A grandfather, a father, a dream, a childhood. Each life story reflected a struggle to come to terms with death and to find some solace in the promise of a new beginning: "I will be like you grandfather, a great medicine woman, a song in my heart, and a medicine bag to call my own."

A third theme, the notion of alienation, also found its way into each story. Marcus tells us that as a child he felt isolated from his mother and father. They never had time for him, would not listen to him, told him he was not important. Clara writes of her struggles trying to live in two worlds, each pulling her farther and farther away from herself. Maia reminds us we are never ready to be orphans.

The fourth theme touched on a more positive note. All of the storytellers claim they experienced some degree of healing through the process of writing their lives. Marcus says, "Understand that simply writing our stories doesn't always heal things completely, but it goes a long way in that process." Clara believes that by writing her struggles in her journal and crafting them into public pieces she "gains a sense of peace and comes to a place of healing in her heart." Maia says the process of writing about her father's death was very painful but also very healing: "It gave me a chance to get down and get out what I didn't get down or out when my dad was still alive."

This whole notion of healing is rather obscure. It is hard to identify and harder to document. The kind of healing we witness here manifests itself in the appearance of some personal growth or change directly related to the writing process. The *healing* these individuals have experienced comes in the form of an awakening or to a new way of looking at a situation, or of finding a sense of closure and acceptance, or even coming to a place where they can find forgiveness and understanding for those things that make us human.

Writer Response Theory

In this book I introduce a notion closely related to Reader Response, that of *Writer Response,* for the purpose of exploring what things happen to a person as the result of writing and sharing his or her stories. What transformations occur?

I preface my discussion of Writer Response with a brief description of the closely related concepts of Reader Response Theory. Considerable contributions appear in the literature on the particulars of Reader Response. Simply put, the definition of Reader Response Theory is that reading is the process of constructing meaning through the dynamic interaction among the reader's existing knowledge, the information suggested by the written language, and the context of the reading situation. Theorists such as Freund, Giroux, Iser, Rosenblatt, and Barone believe that there is a relationship between the reader, the author, and the text. Barone (1995), in an article entitled "Persuasive Writings, Vigilant Readings, and Reconstructed Characters: The Paradox of Trust in Educational Storytelling" stated, "The reality of the text resides within the interaction between the writer and the reader" (p. 64). Reader Response grapples with what things happen to the reader as a result of reading—again, which transformations occur.

Writer Response is a theory I have introduced for consideration by those who are willing to entertain the idea that writing, like reading, is a process of constructing meaning or of making sense of one's stories and experiences. I define it to be the interaction between the writer and the process of writing his or her stories. Like Reader Response, it has to do with a person's existing self, the self that emerges from the experience of writing, and the self that begins to look at the world through different eyes. It suggests the possibility of some change or cathartic episode in a person as a result of writing and sharing personal narratives. If we think in terms of this concept, the question becomes "What transformations or changes in the human conditions have occurred in the three fellow travelers as a result of their journey down the river of their writing and being?" To allow us to answer this question and also consider the implications, we must return to the stories themselves. In the stories we must look for signs of change—any growth or forgiveness or reconciliation of the spirit—that can be attributed to the practice of writing personal narratives.

The concept of Writer Response lays foundation for framing the question, "How does writing and sharing personal narratives change lives?" Earlier in this chapter I looked at the stories of three respondents for answers to this question by evaluating how ENG 494 *Writing and Being* impacted their lives and thinking, and the pondering importance of storytelling as a central element of a writing curriculum.

When I refer to the transformational attributes of storytelling I mean the qualities of personal narrative that may effect a change in the writer, audience, or both—*Writer Response*. References to this notion are abundant and serve to support the thesis of this inquiry.

Educational theorists are beginning to look at the use of narrative storytelling as a credible means of changing lives in schools, clinics, and even in the privacy of a personal journal. In a discussion of narrative as text, Riessman (cited by Shafer, 1992) stated, "Psychologists encounter narratives of personal experience every day and use them to change lives by retelling and constructing new and more fulfilling ones" (p. 2). Riessman (cited by Shafer, 1992) went on to say, "Social movements aid individuals to name their injuries, connect with others, and engage in political action. Research interviewers can also bear witness" (p. 4).

Most curriculum designers, researchers, and theorists are slow to embrace the use of storytelling because it tends to break the mold of traditional thinking. It is somewhat different—possibly even suspect. The subjectivity in narrative causes both a sense of freedom and uneasiness—freedom in that some of the rules are relaxed and the writer has some license but uneasiness because of believability (credibility of source, text, and events). Riessman (cited by Shafer, 1992) suggested, "Subjectivity, of course, is deeply distrusted in mainstream social science, which values context-free laws and generalized explanations" (p. 5).

I have found that in my reading, many scholars believe the transformational power of stories is central to better understanding ourselves and others.

> The power of narrative and dialogue as contributors to reflective awareness in teachers and students is that they provide opportunities for deepened relations with others and serve as springboards for ethical action. Understanding the narrative and contextual dimensions of human actors can lead to new insights, compassionate judgment, and a creation of shared knowledge and meaning that can inform professional practice. (Witherell & Noddings, 1991, p. 8)

McEwan and Egan (1995) said of the transformative function of stories:

> The most rudimentary of all stories designed to transform, as opposed to inform, must surely be the fable. Consider, for example, the ancient stories of the "Tortoise and the Hare," or "The Fox and the Grapes," each with its tacked-on moral. Why introduce either to a classroom full of ten-year-olds? The answer is obvious. The chief reason for doing so is to suggest to the youthful listeners that one way of behaving is more prudent than another. The fable, in other words, resembles a fancy piece of embroidery whose ornamental stitching embellishes a simple moral message. The hope is that the message will not simply be heard and understood but will be taken to heart. (p. 9)

Witherell and Noddings (1991) added to this thought:

> The creative use of story and dialogue lends power to educational and therapeutic experiences because of their capacity to expand our horizons of understanding and provide rich contextual information about human actors,

intentions, and experiences. . . . The individual achieves personhood through caring relation with the other, yet the story of a life is always, in every moment, distinctive from the stories of other lives. (p. 79)

McEwan and Egan (1995) proposed that narratives were a valuable transformational tool in that they "allow us to understand the world in new ways and help us to communicate new ideas to others" (p. 34). If writing and telling our stories can be transformational, change us in some way as these researchers suggest, then might storytelling somehow heal emotional wounds? There is evidence to this emerging belief in the literature. Linda Hogan (1995) wrote, "Story is at the very crux of healing, at the very heart of ceremony and ritual in older America" (p. 37). Emily Nye (1997) told of a recent study at the New Mexico Institute of Mining and Technology where researchers explored the possibility that writing could have healing effects. An AIDS clinic became the site of the research where patients began writing and sharing the stories of their lives and in the process, enjoyed some physical and emotional relief from the devastation of the illness.

I especially like what Susan Albert (1996) believes about writing personal narratives:

> This storytelling work—and it is difficult, demanding work—is remarkably, rewardingly healthy. As we reveal ourselves in story, we become aware of the continuing core of our lives under the fragmented surface of our experiences. As we become conscious of the multifaceted, multichaptered "I" who is the storyteller, we can trace out the paradoxical and even contradictory versions of ourselves that we create for different occasions, different audiences—and the threads that weave all these chapters, all these versions into the whole. Most important, as we become aware of ourselves as storytellers, we realize that what we understand and imagine about ourselves is a story. It is only one way of representing our experiences, of composing and recomposing our lives. Our stories are not the experiences themselves. This realization is deeply healing. (p. 4)

Barry Lopez (cited by Witherell & Noddings, 1991), quoted in the book *Stories Lives Tell*, stated, "The power of narrative to nurture and heal, to repair a spirit in disarray, rests on two things: (1) the skillful invocation of unimpeachable sources and (2) the listener's knowledge that no hypocrisy or subterfuge is involved" (p. 5).

Susan Wanner (1994) wrote:

> People crave stories. Human beings learn and grow in their ability to deal with the world when they participate imaginatively in experience shaped by

art. This narrative truth is moral, not objective; every listener is unique and each derives value from the story according to his or her own needs. (p. 15)

I have used words like *changing* and *healing* frequently in this text. I believe them to be the very substance of my definition of *Writer Response*. The point of this thinking is to fit the promise of healing the human condition with the writing process. One of the strongest endorsements connecting transformation and personal narrative is also the most succinct. In 1958 Isak Dinesen wrote, "Again this is the point—there can be a change in people if stories are allowed to emerge. All sorrows can be borne if we put them into story" (cited by Riessman, 1993, p. 4). References supporting the belief that storytelling is a valuable component of human existence are abundant.

Now, let us return to the stories of Maia and Clara and Marcus to look for changes in their lives, evidence of Writer Response.

Marcus Brown came to *Writing and Being* carrying the heavy burden of hatred inside him. The bitter resentment toward his father sat on fertile ground, fed on Marcus' memories of his chaotic family life. Remember that Marcus said, "I had a whole bunch of stuff buried inside me that I didn't even know about—stuff that was really hurting me—maybe even killing me." By working in his "journal book" and allowing his stories to emerge, Marcus was able to discard much of the hatred that consumed his life. Through the explorations, he wrote of his childhood and was able to identify the cause of his father's treatment of him and even began to empathize with his condition. We saw the violent images in "Being a Child in My Parents' Home" soften a little in the words of "Saw My Father in a Dream." Marcus was discovering the power of writing his pain and learning how to let it go. By the time we see "The Dolphin," Marcus had shed the heavy baggage of hatred and had found a measure of peace as he "began to wonder who we were." Through the real writing process, Marcus stated he found a tool to help save himself.

Clara Bee, the medicine woman, sat in the lamp-lit shadows of an English Department office telling me the stories of her young life. During our informal chats, her hands would dance in the air as if to accompany her conversation. When she read the pieces about her grandfathers and families, her voice and her hands grew quiet. She read "My Grandfather's Medicine Bag" as one would read a prayer, the pain of it etching her soft voice. She tells me that whenever she reads this piece she becomes closer to her grandfather and the grief she feels because of his loss becomes less severe. In the Native culture, a person is never gone if you can still see his face. The words of this "picture" Clara wrote of her grandfather captures his image perfectly. She says that this piece has become a great comfort to her when she is alone and missing home.

Clara feels the pieces that she crafted about the ravages of alcoholism have helped her understand her Native fathers. She is quick to say that while she cannot accept this weakness in her culture, her writing has helped to identify some of the reasons it occurs.

One of the biggest problems Clara brought to *Writing and Being* was the confusion and difficulty that living in two very different worlds brought her. She told us, "It's hard being here in this culture trying to cope with the demands of this school and this society, and trying to maintain my Native heritage at the same time." The prayer called "Little Ones" is one way Clara found to make sense of the conflicts she faces.

At Arizona State University Clara belongs to a group called Native Images. This group of Native people shares its stories at conferences, seminars, conventions, and classrooms all over the United States. Clara has read the stories she included in this project many times. Each time she does, she says she comes a little closer to understanding herself, her relations, and the direction she wants her life to take.

Maia Huntley discovered that through the writing process she could forgive herself and those close to her and begin to move toward a more positive way of seeing her world. She gives herself permission to be imperfect and to understand that her frustrations with her family and her teaching do not necessarily equate to failure.

Maia also carried tremendous guilt in the folds of her heart. She felt guilty for not being with her father when he passed away, and for her negative attitude toward her students. Much of her guilt and frustrations and pain dissolved as a result of her stories. In "Words Unspoken" she found a way to send a silent message to her father, saying words only her heart could say. Writing "Annie Jo" helped gain a better understanding of her aunt and remember her in a positive light. "Maestra" helped affirm Maia's own worth as a teacher—a struggling novice who is making amazing accomplishments. Maia says she is at a very different place as a result of writing the stories of her life. Her spirit and attitude have healed. She has recovered a part of herself that she thought was lost forever. She believes strongly in the value of narrative storytelling as an approach that could solve many social and emotional problems throughout the human community.

Each storyteller revealed that through the process of writing and sharing their stories, he or she has realized some change—some transformation in their lives. They let go of hatred, learned to grieve and mourn, survived the threat of alienation, gave voice to frustrations, and captured precious memories. What these people brought to the table the first night of class and what they took from it the last night become the delicate stone we can hold up to the light.

So let us look back at this chapter. The very nature of qualitative inquiry suggests that we begin to ask more questions than we answer. In this chapter we have found some answers and perhaps generated even more questions for consideration. In keeping with the function of *Fourth Generation Evaluation* (Guba & Lincoln, 1989), we have taken a look at the claims, concerns, and issues of the stakeholders involved as part of the evaluation of this writing program. I have also introduced the concept of *Writer Response* theory for consideration and offered some support for its notions through the literature. I have identified several common themes that emerged during the research by retelling passages of the stories.

As a passionate participant in this text, I serve only to bring glimpses of truth and reality before you to hold up to the light of evaluation. None of the transformations reported within the context of this study can be proven or disproven. They are "human mental conditions" (Guba & Lincoln, 1989, p. 21), offered as food for thought to those of us who are in some position to affect the course of educational direction. It behooves us to consider the possibilities for curricular and instructional design carefully.

FIVE

Evolution and Exploration

The Conceptual Journey of Narrative Based Evaluation

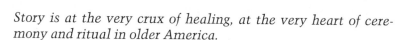

Story is at the very crux of healing, at the very heart of cere-mony and ritual in older America.

—*Linda Hogan, 1995, p. 37*

Winfield Bennett and his wife are working parents who are concerned about their son coming home to an empty house every day after school. There is a program at the elementary school that allows children to be supervised until parents get off work and can come for them. Children can get help with homework, play games, rest, and even get a snack. The Bennetts want to find out from the school staff and other parents the benefits and effectiveness of this program.

Margaret Curry is a local artist who sees a need to get children involved in reading and art through her work at the public library. She wants to find out about the possibilities of beginning a program that will integrate literature and art into a meaningful experience for children.

Lourdes Vallejo is a parent of a child who attends a year-round school. She is concerned about the times during intersession when children do not have school but parents still have to work. Lourdes is considering opening a day care program during the intersession weeks but needs information and help with organization. She plans to investigate the possibilities of a program such as this by talking to officials in other school districts who have similar pro-grams in place.

The purpose of this chapter is to explore the conceptual roots of *Narrative Based Evaluation*. I begin by looking at some of the ideas associated with educational evaluation. Then, like Clara's grandmother sitting at her loom, I weave these ideas into the philosophical framework of interpretivism, formative evaluation, and responsive constructive evaluation into the fabric of this project. Think of this rug woven by Clara's grandmother as a representation of where we have been.

So we continue our journey—the journey whose ultimate destination was to ponder my question, "Does writing and sharing personal narratives change lives?" As we wind our way through the multifaceted cutbanks of this river, keep your own story in mind. Keep Marcus, Maia, and Clara in mind, too. They are on this adventure with us and are some of the intended beneficiaries of our theoretical designs.

Educational Evaluation

Every watery ripple that splashed our craft during this journey down the river of our writing and our being reflected the purpose of our trip and our understanding of the power of narrative storytelling. By evaluating the course *Writing and Being*—by looking at its value in terms of its curricular design and function—I am able to offer the opportunity to rethink some traditional practices to educators and others who directly impact the direction of schools and schooling.

In each of the scenarios that prefaced this chapter, someone was seeking information that would attach a measure of worthiness or credibility to a program and to the participants of that program—its stakeholders. Mr. and Mrs. Bennett are thinking about entrusting their child to those in charge of an after-school program. As concerned parents, they need solid information before making a decision that will impact their lives. Ms. Curry wants to enhance a literature program by offering artistic experiences for children. But first she must consider the value of such a program in terms of student interest, financial concerns, and community support. The opportunity to begin a small business is appealing to Lourdes Vallejo. The need is apparent but Lourdes needs to do considerable investigation before committing herself and others to this program. During my research for this book I looked at the curriculum of a writing course based on narrative storytelling and used the interpretation of that curriculum by three course participants, its beneficiaries, as the substance of my perspective in guiding the evaluation.

Guba and Lincoln (1989) wrote:

Evaluation outcomes are not descriptions of the "way things really are" or "really work," or of some "true" state of affairs, but instead represent meaningful constructions that individual actors or groups of actors form to make sense of the situations in which they find themselves. (p. 8)

This belief is foundational to our explorations here. Marcus, Clara, and Maia believe they have realized some amount of change in their personal lives that is directly related to their involvement in *Writing and Being.*

The underlying purpose of any evaluation is to make a judgment of goodness about a practice, program, project, or even a person. Simply put, evaluation is about valuing (Scriven, 1967) and judging (Stake, 1967). A program evaluation brings into question the quality and effectiveness of stated purposes or intentions by those in position to render sound judgments. Many educators understand the importance of evaluating programs that directly impact students' and teachers' lives. Let us think about some of those students for a minute. By the time our lives collide in class, they (students) are often exposed to a myriad of educational programs, most promising miraculous results, and most thrust upon them with a reckless disregard for their particular situation. My teaching colleagues and I laughingly used to call these "canned programs" because of their generic "one-size-fits-all" propaganda. One must ask, with home situations and opportunities aside, how are our students helped academically, socially, and emotionally by years of involvement in the educational system? Central to my work here is the value people place on their lived experiences. Throughout my investigation we have seen how personal reflection through the writing process offers us insights into the way we look at the episodes of our lives. Interpretivism is the research equivalent to this work as a load-bearing wall is to the construction of a building. It acts as the support structure for the study. In fact, Denzin and Lincoln (1994) supported the idea that "all research is interpretive, guided by a set of beliefs and feelings about the world and how it should be understood and studied" (p. 13). Working within an interpretive paradigm, researchers construct and reconstruct meaning (make sense) of the world, using the light caught in the prisms of their own experiences. This study has evolved into an interpretation of the transformational effects of narrative storytelling.

As Denzin and Lincoln (1994) wrote, "At root, interpretivism is about contextualized meaning" (p. 536). We, as human beings, constantly recreate our versions of truth or reality and make sense of the world around us through the interpretation of our lived experiences.

Given our proclivity to continually redefine ourselves, whatever knowledge and understanding we acquire through this process are temporary. What we know of reality is never static but ever-changing as the autobiography of the self struggles to emerge. "Reality resides neither with an objective external world nor with the subjective mind of the knower, but with the dynamic transactions between the two" (Barone, 1992b, p. 31). It is this continuous interplay between the mind and the outside world—these phenomenological episodes—that seats this work squarely in the center of interpretivist logic.

Interpretivism promotes qualities of understanding, awareness, and diverse perspectives. These values play foundational roles in the storied lives represented in the journey of this study. Marcus has gained a more insightful understanding of his relationship with his father. Clara has learned to survive the demands of university life while maintaining strong ties to her Navajo culture. And Maia has become more aware of talents she possesses in teaching troubled children.

Interpretivism allows human beings continually to redefine versions of reality or truth. We have seen this through the storied lives represented in this study. Marcus, Clara, and Maia were able to locate different versions of the truth (versions of their reality) in every account included in their journeys. Through their personal narratives they changed perspectives and attitudes and even softened the pain of traumatic events in their lives. The things that were once so "real" continued to change and evolve through the process of discovery.

It is this process of constant self-discovery or self-evaluation that connects the notions of interpretivism with those of formative evaluation. Michael Scriven first used the term *formative evaluation* in 1967 in an essay entitled "The Countenance of Educational Evaluation" (cited by Bloom, 1971). In this essay, he noted that formative evaluation is a form of evaluation that encourages stakeholders to think about the practices they employ and possibly modify them to accommodate improvement and success. He wrote that, in part, "formative evaluation involves the collection of appropriate evidence during the construction and trying out of a new curriculum in such a way that revisions of the curriculum can be based on this evidence" (p. 135). Formative evaluation is supposed to make people think about what they are doing. I crafted this inquiry to reflect the understanding of this definition of formative evaluation because I believe there is a great need for educators to rethink traditional curricular design.

Let us take a closer look at what formative evaluation suggests. Bloom (1971, cited by Witherell & Noddings, 1991) wrote that "formative evaluation is the use of systematic evaluation in the process of curriculum construction, teaching, and learning for the purpose of improving any of these processes" (p. 117). This thinking is closely related to Scriven's concept of evaluation in that educators are encouraged to judge the merit of a practice with the intent of improving its effectiveness. Another connection to the thoughts of Bloom and Scriven can be found in Elliot Eisner's (1985a) functions of educational evaluation. He wrote, "The main functions of educational evaluation are: (1) to diagnose (2) to revise curricula (3) to compare (4) to anticipate educational needs, and (5) to determine if objectives have been met" (p. 192). By revising the curricula and anticipating educational needs we, in the educational community, are seeking to improve practices teachers use in classrooms. Eisner (1985a) continued this thought when he wrote, "What we want education as a process to accomplish is not merely to change students but to improve the quality of their lives" (p. 183).

Formative evaluation is deeply embedded in this book. What I have done is to look at narrative storytelling as an approach that might be used to improve the way teachers connect with children. It is possible that Lynn Nelson might also be a benefactor of this study. Perhaps he has gained some insights and ideas about the structure of *Writing and Being* and how to meet his students' needs. The research that laid the groundwork for this book is also formative in that I presented the content and claims of ENG 494 in relation to my respondents' interpretation of the curriculum to serve as a value of its goodness. Formative evaluation encourages us to ask more questions than we answer. It urges us to consider possibilities about curricular design that are routinely stifled by dispassionate observers who find the "truth" in the results of assessment instruments that are often disconnected from the things students really learn in school.

Through my reading, I found the notions of formative evaluation to be closely related to what Guba and Lincoln (1989) attributed to what Stake (1967) called *responsive constructivist evaluation*. "Robert Stake proposed the notion of responsive evaluation which determines the boundaries and parameters of an investigation through the interactive, negotiated process that involves stakeholders" (Guba & Lincoln, 1989, p. 39). Guba and Lincoln continued:

> Responsive evaluation is not only responsive for the reason that it seeks out different stakeholder views but also since it responds to those items in the subsequent collection of materials. It is quite likely that different stakeholders will hold different constructions with respect to any particular claim, concern, or issue. (p. 41)

Each of my three respondents approached writing his or her Explorations differently, and each took different measures of transformation away from them.

Remember that Marcus, Clara, and Maia are in the boat with us. They are the stakeholders on this journey, the exploration of the river. As stakeholders in the study they are immediate beneficiaries of the writing program and the evaluation I presented here. They participated in the construction of this project by discussing their experiences in the writing course and by offering their personal narratives for my interpretation and evaluation. All of this speaks directly to the value of the writing process as an important component of a language curriculum.

Let us narrow the focus to look at the aspects of narrative that contributed to my conceptualization of *Narrative Based Evaluation.*

Narrative

Webster (*Random House,* 1992) defined narrative as "the telling of a story or the account of events, experiences or the like" (p. 899). The literature of educational research seeks to further explain Webster's definition by delineating narrative's value to the human experience. Some examples of this are as follows:

- A primary act of the mind. (Hardy, 1977, cited by Wilhelm, 1995, p. 20)
- The primary scheme by means of which human existence is rendered meaningful. (Polkinghorne, 1988, cited by Hopkins, 1994, p. 131)
- A means by which human beings represent and restructure the world. (Mitchell, 1981, cited by Cortazzi, 1993, p. 8)
- The organizing principle by which people organize their experience in, knowledge about, and transactions with the social world. (Bruner, 1990, cited by Cortazzi, 1993, p. 1)
- Narrative erupts at the intersection of experience, emotion, and language. (Wanner, 1994, p. 15)

To craft my own definition of this approach, I searched the literature, consulted with colleagues, and reflected upon my experience as an English teacher. In this book, I used *narrative* to refer to the way we tell our stories. It is the form our stories take when we use our language and our own voice to record or tell the experiences of our lives. With this in mind, think of the narrative structure as a mighty river whose tributaries branch forth in a variety of presentations. We, as human beings, record our life experiences in many ways. We write notes and keep journals. We interview people and write letters. We share ourselves with others through biographies and autobiographies. And we write the stories of our lived experiences.

The concept of narrative contributes to telling the stories of our lives. Jean Clandinin and Michael Connelly (cited by Denzin & Lincoln, 1994) described narrative "as both phenomenon and method. Narrative names the structured quality of experience to be studied and it names the pattern of inquiry for the study" (p. 416). Borrowing from this terminology, narrative is therefore both the method and the product of an inquiry. Recall the stories of the three respondents in this study. Marcus, Clara, and Maia offered the written experiences of their lives as narrative accounts constructed for the purposes of illumination, self-growth, and understanding. Their narratives were examples of both method and product.

Petra Munro (1993) also contributed to this view of narrative. She wrote, "How we tell our stories, the narrative form, becomes a window to ways of knowing" (p. 163). This supports the notion that through our narrative storytelling we, as human beings, can come to a better place of knowing ourselves and understanding others. "In narrative work there is a particular emphasis on how we tell our stories rather than what is told" (Munro, 1993, p. 115). Do you remember Lynn Nelson asking that the narrative be allowed to take whatever form it wants? This supports Munro's notion.

Let us explore the subtle distinctions between a life history and a life story. The literature is blurred on differences between the two, so how do we know if narrative structures record the experiences of a person's history or of his story? For the purposes of this research, the term *life story* is defined as a structured account of an individual's life experience. A life history is an interpretation of that story. As Cortazzi (1993) suggested, "A life story is a personal reconstruction of an experience, while a life history draws upon a wider range of evidence: interviews, discussions, relevant texts, and contexts" (p. 14). We can further relate the differences to the notions of biography and autobiography—a biography being a person's life history and an autobiography, his story.

A passage in *The Aims of Interpretation* by E. D. Hirsch (1976) is useful for clarifying the difference between life story and life history. In the introduction of his book, Hirsch explains his interpretation of the terms *meaning* and *significance:* "The term *meaning* refers to the whole verbal meaning of a text, and *significance* to textual meaning in relation to a larger context as in another mind, another era, a wider subject matter—indeed any context beyond itself" (p. 2). This thinking fits closely to Cortazzi (1993) if we equate *meaning* to story and *significance* to history. Both concepts, story and history, are presented here. The stories of the three participants are presented in Chapter 3. Each storyteller offered episodes of his or her life that reflected a pattern of transformation that I interpreted in Chapter 4. I offered my interpretation of their stories through interviews, discussions, and personal narratives to craft life histories for this work.

So how do we tell our stories? I am reminded of the suggestion Lynn Nelson made on one of the explorations presented in this study: "Let it [the narrative] become what it wants or needs to become." Maia, Clara, and Marcus have done just that. The shape and substance of their narratives appear very different; however, all of them are reflections of lived experiences and are evidence of individuals "coming to know" themselves.

Were there surprises in some of the narratives contained within this study? Of course. Surprises respond to the aesthetics of the narrative form. Barone (1997) wrote:

> Good stories, as art, do not conclude, but suggest, eschewing direct summary statements for delicate hints about theme and thesis. Storied texts may surprise the reader who is expecting a traditional form of closure, for rewards are forthcoming only upon strict attention to allusion and nuance and upon the extra effort of the reader to read between the lines. (p. 224)

The reader might have been surprised by Marcus' violent images of his father in "Being a Child in My Parents' Home." You might have read between the lines of "My Grandfather's Medicine Bag" to find Clara's consuming pride in her heritage. You may have felt the crushing grief and guilt to which Maia alluded in "Words Unspoken."

Crafting a narrative means turning our experiences into words. When we shape our experiences into language, they become stories that help us understand ourselves. Connelly and Clandinin (1988) wrote:

> Narrative refers to the making of meaning through personal experience by way of a process of reflection in which storytelling is a key element and in which metaphors and folk knowledge take their place. Situations call forth our images from our narratives of experience, and these images are available to act as guides to future action. (p. 17)

Narratives, including those from educators and children, allow us to learn about ourselves through reflecting on our own experiences.

Each student who walks into every classroom enters with a storied life that will define and guide his or her journey. Each teacher who stands before a class has the opportunity to tap into that reservoir of life stories in an effort to encourage understanding within individuals, the classroom, and ultimately our social worlds.

The autobiography of the self is a powerful tool that is overlooked if curriculum designers narrow the scope of education to only textbooks. The importance of redefining self through autobiography is supported by William Pinar (1988, cited by Cortazzi, 1993):

> Narrative is a strategy to disclose educational experiences. Autobiography, as self-narrative, becomes a method of reflecting on the self in lived experience. Autobiography is an inquiry into the architecture of the self which shows the author how experience has been construed and reveals ways in which the curriculum has helped to grind the perceptual lens of the writer. (p. 12)

We, as teachers, ask students to define vocabulary words and learn how to use them. But do we also ask our students to define themselves? The architecture of the self reflects one's emerging definition. Narrative storytelling, the practice of writing our stories, allows us to define and redefine ourselves. It allows us the privilege of reconstructing the way we think—the way we process the events of our lives.

Along this journey, both the researcher and reader have looked at the purpose of evaluation in terms of some judgment of goodness, and explored the promise of personal narrative as a way of knowing ourselves and others. Now let us direct our attention toward the concept of *Narrative Based Evaluation* and its place in educational research.

Narrative Based Evaluation

This study is an example of *Narrative Based Evaluation*. I offer it to the research community as a way of thinking about program evaluation which uses narrative as a tool for both the focus and form of presentation. Deeply embedded in this conceptual structure is the premise that narrative accounts can be revealed and utilized as both product and method. My aim has been to develop the concept of *Narrative Based Evaluation* for future consideration in educational discourse.

Connelly and Clandinin (cited by Denzin & Lincoln, 1994) wrote, "People by nature lead storied lives, whereas narrative researchers describe such lives, collect and tell stories of them, and write narratives of experience" (p. 416). Both assumptions are represented in this text as stories and histories. What I have done here is to evaluate ENG 494, *Writing and Being*, by using the same approach employed in the class—that of narrative storytelling.

Let us return, one last time, to the river of our exploration of *Narrative Based Evaluation*. If people do indeed lead storied lives and are all storytelling creatures, what can be said for the purpose of these actions? Consider this. The very act of storytelling is an act of evaluation. In order to look at the episodes in our lives, we must move from an experience to a reflection upon the experience—a story. We take ourselves out of the water, into a boat, and onto the banks of the river, to become observers of our experiences—outside where we are able to make choices about the experiences, to own them or to let them go. This is where we are able to evaluate them. Our language allows us to get outside our experiences. It is a tool for making sense of the world and to find meaning in our lives. Therefore, when an experience moves into a story, it becomes, by its very nature, evaluation.

Lynn Nelson (1994) made reference to this point in Chapter 5 of *Writing and Being: Taking Back Our Lives Through the Power of Language*. He wrote:

> The key to the transformational power of this writing process, then, is something like this: As I write about my anger, I am watching my anger. If I am watching my anger, then the anger is only one part of me, not all of me. I am not trapped in it. I am not my anger. I may have anger, but I am not my anger. There is a great and crucial difference between having anger and being anger. When I am my anger, when it consumes me, when I cannot watch it, watch the "I" that is angry, then that "I," or that angry self is in control. Then the rest of me has no choices but its choices. I am at the mercy of my anger. Then I cannot act; I can only react. (p. 78)

Without this process of telling our stories, we are trapped in our experiences. Remember Marcus? In his story he said, "Because I can write about the hurt I have experienced, I begin to realize that I have choices—choices regarding the baggage I want to carry and what I want to let go." And later in his story, he wondered how things might have been different for him if his father had kept a journal book.

This is the substance of this book. I have told a story—about a class—about people telling stories. I have been in the river with my own writing and with Marcus, and Clara, and Maia as they dared to dance the tides with me. I have made my way to the banks of the river, still wet from my swim, to look back on my experiences and those who swam with me. From the banks of the river I wrote the story of my journey into *Writing and Being.* Throughout this whole process, I was affirmed in my belief that there is great power in stories, power that can change our lives and help us find our way, power that can help us heal our wounded hearts and spirits and arrive at a clearer understanding of the world, and power to help ease the struggles of the children in our classrooms.

I close with this thought from Sam Keen and Anne Valley Fox (1973):

> We invent stories about the origin and conclusion of life because we are exiles in the middle of time. The void surrounds us. We live within the parentheses surrounded by question marks. Our stories and myths do not dispel ignorance, but they help us find our way, our place at the heart of the mystery. In the end, as in the beginning, there will be a vast silence, broken by the sound of one person telling a story to another. (p. 151)

SIX

When You Hold a Crystal to the Light

The Educative Implications of Narrative Based Evaluation

⌒

Let the story in. — *Titanic (The Movie)*

Shards of Illumination

When I was a young girl I loved to catch sunlight in crystals and watch as colors once trapped in invisibility burst forth in kaleidoscopic magic. In this chapter I seek to explicate the nature of *Narrative Based Evaluation* by offering three examples of pedagogical application. As light traveling through a prism is refracted in many directions and intensities, so too is the evocative nature of using the constructs of narrative when we think about program evaluation.

So let me revisit the spirit of this work and how I look at it as a formative approach for educational enlightenment as well as a metaphorical footbridge between inquiry, theory, and practice. Appropriate here is to look at what Guba and Lincoln (1989) say in terms of responsive constructivist evaluation and the considerable involvement of its stakeholders. They say:

> Evaluation outcomes are not descriptors of the "way things really are" or "really work," or of some "true" state of affairs, but instead represent meaningful constructions that individual actors or groups of actors form to "make sense" of the situations in which they find themselves. (Guba & Lincoln, 1989, p. 8)

At the beginning of this work I stated that storytelling, in its many representations, can have the power to enliven and awaken the way educators formulate curriculum design, application, and assessment. I believe there is no better way to authenticate this belief than to provide documentation by stakeholders who have been touched in some way by the notion that through the process of writing and sharing stories we possess the provocative power of understanding. Moreover, this process is synergistic in its breadth, fertile with possibilities for personal transformation, and timeless in necessity. It is tantamount to wording toward the light.

So we will continue our journey by looking at three instances where *Narrative Based Evaluation* serves as both the form and focus of curriculum design, practice, and inquiry.

Drenched in the Light

Katherine Griffith is a middle school teacher in inner-city Phoenix, Arizona. I first met Katherine three years ago when she was a student in my qualitative research class which was part of her program of study for a doctoral degree in Educational Leadership and Policy Studies. One of the course requirements of the class was to conduct an Action Research project and present the findings to the class. Katherine and her group chose to look at the notion of pride and how it is manifested in children's narrative reflections. Her initial efforts in action research became the foundation for her doctoral thesis and subsequent dissertation. Here is her story:

> *Narrative Based Evaluation* has had a momentous effect on my life and my ability to process, internalize and make use of damaging experiences in a productive way. In truth, I see it as an art of healing. I was first introduced to *Narrative Based Evaluation* when I took Dr. Marsha Harrison's qualitative research class in the fall of 1999. I was struck by the honesty in the approach and the connections I made with my students when we shared and reacted to our writing pieces mutually.
>
> I remember one particular afternoon I read a journal entry to my students about a childhood memory of my brother and the alienation I felt living so far from him and his family. I became so overwhelmed by their [students'] acceptance of me and what I had to say about someone very special in my life. I was afraid to look up or keep reading because I didn't want them to see the wailing in

my eyes or hear the fracture in my voice. The slippery giant of emotion that gripped my throat with thick, tight, muscular fingers surprised me as much as it surprised them. "Go on Mrs. Griffith, it's okay," I heard a small voice whisper. It was hard to believe I had little fourth and fifth graders urging me to be myself and let down my guards. I struggled in that moment for what seemed to be a fraction of infinity as twenty-five hushed voices smuggled me their tidbits of encouragement. I was able to finally finish and the applause they gave me when I was finished sounded like the thunderous praise of a *Grammy* packed audience.

It was as though both the experience of taking qualitative research and discovering the power of the story as well as the intimate exchange I had experienced with my class combined to prompt me to write a piece with an absymal storyline that is unfortunately true. When I was Marsha Harrison's student I could often feel the rippling surges of magnetic energy she gave off that told me how fervent her zeal for teaching and writing was. She helped remind me how much power both good and bad teachers have to impact lives with just a few words.

The most pivotal part of the class for me was when Dr. Harrison gave the class an assignment to write about a true event in our childhood that stood out in our minds. She encouraged us to be as descriptive as possible. I decided to carve out the bleeding details surrounding an incident that still pulsates in red—even now after so many years—even now when I am so happy. It was an occurrence that slashed my childhood savagely leaving it to resemble the displaced stuffing of a Raggedy Ann doll. I didn't like the room being a victim occupied, even in the best hiding places in my mind and I was so very relieved to finally get it out, put it down on paper, put it somewhere that made sense in a story, which is the most therapeutic, light-filled place I know.

This experience and others led me to begin writing my life, the writing often taking the form of poetry. I see poetry as a vehicle which helps transport me along my journey and helps me to find my way peacefully. I wrote this poem as a sort of healing exercise because I so often feel a great sadness teaching children with disadvantaged lives. It is a curious combination of sadness but also of the pride I feel being black and female. This poem is dedicated to what I value and perceive as beauty as well as my expression of my failure to be suppressed.

BLACK ON THE INSIDE

On the outside
I'm so cool
Just as pastel as sandpaper
I can even use the Maybelline
Face powder the white girls use

But deep down where
My heart pumps hard and fast
Deep down where babies are made
And carried
I'm bottomless, dark
And black
Sooty like the scorched
Underside of Mama's good pot
Its cracked, mottled
Cast iron shell
Gives existence to succulent
Concoctions

Just like my presence
Favors a room
With hints of bronze
And teeth
And hips
And oozing belly laughter
Drawn from way down
At the bottom of the well
Black on the inside
Charred and pretty
Hot and sticky

On the surface
I'm delicate
Speaking good
Proper English
I pretend to say all the right things
But the inflection is all wrong
My smile is off cue
To the trained eye

I'm boiling over

Tar sweat beads
At the top of my brow
Pitch edges over
The slit of my eyes
And shadowed the
Bubbling beneath
The soul
The rocking and
Quaking
The making of me
Black on the inside

My doctoral research, *Searching for Light: Finding Voices of Pride Through Narrative and Poetic Expression*, explored the power of narrative, as manifestations of pride in students and the impact of writing on students' personal lives. The purpose of my study was to help illuminate teaching environments and strategies that foster the expression of internal voice in students. I also wanted to look at the relationship between storied lives and the effect of poetic and narrative expression on self-concept.

I used phenomenological episodes in students' lives which served to enhance or approach a transformation of some degree. I asked them to write honestly about themselves and their experiences thus to come to a clearer understanding of themselves in the process. My students were interviewed regarding specific writing experiences in the classroom that evoked feelings of pride or a lack thereof. Simply put, I used Narrative Based Evaluation to examine the journey that each person experienced while finding, writing, and using his or her inner voice.

What of the implications of using Narrative Based Evaluation on in the classroom? What food for thought does it offer for educators? How can we begin to change our thinking with regard to assessment? One answer to these questions may be found in the way we can change violent attitudes and behaviors to peaceful ones through the process of writing. I had to encourage tolerance of diversity. But more than that we found a way to celebrate it, to allow room for varied ways of self-expression and respect throughout the community of learners.

Recently during graduation ceremonies, after I hooded her with her doctoral colors, after she walked across the stage to receive her diploma, Katherine gave me a gift. It was the gift of one of her life stories, which she feels has helped greatly to define and demythologize who she is. It was a beautifully framed copy of *Black on the Inside*.

Reflection and Response

Now let us turn our attention to the use of *Narrative Based Evaluation* in terms of formative program evaluation. At the university one of my responsibilities is to act as academic coordinator for a postbaccalaureate program in secondary education. This program, Integrated Certification In Teacher Education (INCITE) offers degreed working professionals the opportunity to return to school to meet the requirements of obtaining a teaching certificate. The program is new to our campus and at the end of the semester I offered my instructors, students, and colleagues the opportunity to share in the evaluation process. Following are the instruments I used to elicit responses.

April 2, 2001

Dear INCITE Colleagues,

As Academic Coordinator for INCITE Secondary, I am interested in how you think things are going. By now you have taught one course or have acted as a facilitator for the program in some way and you have some good information that will help make this program stronger. Using the genre of narrative please respond to these notions:

- Was this a good experience for your students and/or yourself
- Did curriculum meet the needs of the students
- What are some of the things that seemed to be going especially well
- What are some things you feel need more attention
- In general are students focused and enthusiastic
- In terms of textbooks are you and the students being served satisfactorily
- In your opinion are we meeting students' needs

- Are you satisfied with location of classes and facilities in general
- What are your suggestions to improve the program

I encourage you to spend some time with this as I believe your input to be a valuable contribution to the evaluation and improvement of this program.

Thank you in advance for your consideration of this.

Marsha D. Harrison

The following is a response from one of the instructors.

MY IMPRESSIONS ON OUR FIRST SEMESTER.

This semester has gone by so quickly and I don't think I did nearly half of what I intended to do. As far as my class is concerned, I think things went fairly well but that opinion may not be completely shared by my students. They seem to be so overwhelmed by problems outside my classroom that they feel frustrated. I think many times this frustration spills over into the things I have planned for the evening. They seem to feel the need to vent or share stories about situations involving players in the program— some complimentary, some not. But I feel compelled to listen to them regardless. For some unknown reason they think I have answers to many of their concerns.

Textbooks and materials were accessible and appropriate for my class. While we did not have time to completely explore the material, I relied on students to familiarize themselves with concepts and literature we couldn't cover in class. Given the chance, I will use the same textbook next semester.

Location and facilities were okay but the students had a hard time finding drinks and water after the custodians locked us in when their shift was over for the evening. I understand the need for security but many of my students came directly from work without dinner of any kind. It would be nice if there could be soda and snack machines close by to see them through until they could get home. On a better note the classroom was wonderful. The TV/VCR made it very convenient for showing videos related to my curriculum. The room provided a clean and welcoming environment.

Something to think about would be to not have the classes run so late in the evening. I'm not sure what the other instructors are feeling but trying to keep attention and focused discussions until 9:30 is nearly impossible. Most of the students start glazing over before nine. Maybe we could think about offering the classes an hour earlier—4:30 rather than 5:30. Any way you slice it, four hours is a long time to concentrate after someone has worked all day. Just a thought.

All in all though things did seem to work well. I think the students had a pretty good experience and I am happy for the most part. This is a great group of students. They seem to know what they want to do and are eager to jump into the profession of teaching.

I hope this helps. Let me know if you have further concerns or questions. Thanks for the opportunity to share my thoughts on the first semester of INCITE.

The following survey went out to students in the program.

INCITE

PROGRAM EVALUATION

Please respond to these questions in narrative form. We are looking to evaluate the program from the students' perspective as we complete the first semester.

1. How is the course format working for you (9 week classes—4 hours each night)? _____

   _____

   _____

   _____

2. Talk about the curriculum and the courses you have taken so far. What have you learned? Are we meeting your needs? _____

   _____

   _____

   _____

3. Think about the instruction you have been receiving. Is it generally effective? _____

_____
_____
_____

4. In your opinion what are some of the strengths of the program?
_____
_____
_____

5. How do you think we could improve the INCITE program and make it more effective? _____
_____
_____
_____

We value your thoughts and appreciate your contribution to the success of this program.

Thank you,
Marsha D. Harrison

The last *shard of light* is a story I wrote about one of my former students.

THE DARK IN GRACIE'S EYES

She had just finished her 15th summer at the beginning of that school year. Hating where she found herself, she absently handed her class schedule to me and quickly slipped into a back row seat in my eighth grade English class. I could already tell that Gracie's mood was as dark as her eyes. In spite of the heavy makeup and the brood of her pouty stare, she appeared fragile, oddly old, something glasslike. I remember believing that she saw in me just another in a long string of teachers who would aim stones at her, who would try by any means available to break the delicate child wrapped in such provocative trimmings. Or even worse, ignore her altogether. And the thought occurred to me, had this child of glass already been cracked or chipped or broken—broken beyond repair?

Gracie had only one agenda for school and it had nothing to do with learning, making friends, being a teenager, or even being liked. She was here simply to put in her time. Twice retained and just recently released from a correctional center, this was it for her. From her own mouth I had heard that all she wanted was to be out of school, become pregnant, and have a child as soon as possible. The school counselor had left a note in my mailbox saying his advice to me was not to force her to do anything. "Gracie's not a nice girl," the note said, "nothing but trouble. Don't waste your time on her."

Well, I couldn't handle that endearing advice and was therefore resolved to completely ignore it. I started to include Gracie in anything her sour attitude would allow and decided to let the accompanying dirty looks and foul language slide right off me. One day the class began doing some journal work on an exploration called Heart Scars from Lynn Nelson's book. Heart Scars explores emotional wounds—things that we as humans are trained to repress or hide from ourselves and certainly others. I made it clear to the class that this would be private writing—nothing that we would share at that point. Initially Gracie seemed her usual reluctant self and appeared suspicious about participating, but then she did the most amazing thing—she asked for a pencil and a piece of paper.

It was as if her only immediate need was simply to possess the writing material I had just given to her. She positioned the pencil on the top line of the notebook paper and covered it with knitted fingers. This sort of secret ceremony intrigued me—this pressing of palms and pencil and paper. Was she somehow willing her words into print on the flight of thought? Or was she instead denying them life by trying to push them away?

After a while, Gracie's head began a slow descent finally resting on the knuckles of her folded hands. I could see her shoulders begin to jerk in an erratic rhythm that matched her ragged breath. Before too long, black tear droplets were running unchecked from her cheerless eyes, soaking the blank sheet of paper on her desk. She was crying.

To save her from herself, I pretended to need something in the back of the room and dropped a hall pass to the restroom into Gracie's hands as I brushed by. She went unnoticed from the room, leaving her books and purse and the first few thought pages of her untold story lying in rumpled wetness behind.

For the next three days, Gracie's name appeared on the absence list. But by the end of the week she was back. She was back and so was her attitude. Her black mood seemingly redefined during her suspicious absence. While she was gone, I had decided that if she ever did return, I would offer her a slight alternative to the more structured approach to English class. I would simply let her write the stories of her life.

When she came to class on that Friday, she found a note on her desk. It said:

Gracie, there is a journal with your name in it sitting on a table in the pod area. I think it might be a good idea for you to do something a little different for awhile. Maybe you could begin writing about some of the things that are going on in your life—some of the good things—some of the not so good things. Don't worry, I won't read anything in your journal. This will just be private work—Gracie talking to Gracie. If you think you want to try this, I will consider it your participation in my class. The only rules are that you write honestly and tell your stories from your heart. Think about this. Read this note over a few times. And then, if you agree to try this idea, you may get up from your desk and go find your journal. This will be just between us.

Gracie did not make her mind up right away. She just sat there chewing on her bottom lip and refusing to look at me while she considered her options. It was clear that we would play this her way and according to her own need to control the situation. But then, in the time it took me to get the class reading a chapter in *A Separate Peace,* Gracie was gone. She had slipped away into the pod and was reading the words I left for her on a sticky note attached to the first page of her journal. They were the same questions Maia thought about in her initial position paper: How are you feeling about yourself right now? What things are you struggling with? What things are going right in your life? What things are hurting you? What makes you smile? What makes you cry? What things need to be changed? For the rest of the hour, she did exactly what I hoped she would do—just sit and think and wonder.

Later, as she made her way out the door, Gracie made sure I could see the sunflowered jacket of her journal tucked between her math and science books. But the flat line of her dark red lips suggested the conspiracy was to stay just between us.

During the days and weeks that followed, Gracie's journal work would come in episodes of fevered scribbling and times when she would simply be still within herself, reflecting, wording her way around some chapter in thought only. And this is how she spent her time in my English class—doing the solitary work of mending her broken wings. I could tell that she regarded her individual curriculum as very serious business. It was something she owned and treasured. She never took advantage of her freedom from routine lessons nor did she feel compelled to explain anything to her friends.

As Gracie immersed herself in the waters of her writing, I began to notice subtle changes in her attitude, her behavior, and her appearance. She started offering me a tentative "hi" as she came into class and her usual "Why don't you just drop dead?" looks were being replaced by something approaching amiability. There was also a softening in the edges of her stony countenance. Whatever changes were happening on the inside began showing up on the outside, too. Her pretty face bore less of the heavy gothic makeup and she was starting to trade her hard street-wise look for the basic simplicity of a 15-year-old. She began plaiting her dark hair into a thick rope that hung down her back and showed off the natural widow's peak on her forehead. Gracie seemed like a much happier person. She appeared more comfortable with her looks and her identity. She was approaching a more peaceful place within her young soul.

One day in November, the old Gracie came to my class. Her mood was foul. Her delicate face once again varnished in drug store color. Her hair was full around her face and stiffened hard with spray. She wore black clothes from head to toe and something else—something heartbreaking. A dark plum-sized bruise, the kind no amount of makeup could cover, tarnished the elegant lines of her Yaqui cheekbone. Two fingers on her right hand were splinted and taped together, the tips blue and swollen. A very noticeable limp slowed the usual spirited pace I had come to enjoy. I asked a thousand questions in the awkward silence of my helpless stare. She answered my questions in a heartbeat as tears spilled over her dark, gritty lashes. I could only watch, stunned and paralyzed, as this gentle child's cautious footfalls took her into the safety of the pod. I watched as she eased her stiff body into the chair, fumbled in her backpack for her journal, and located a blank page. Then she balanced a pencil in the threads of her three remaining good fingers, and began writing. In some convolution of thought, it occurred to me that Gracie's hand almost looked like it could be holding a cup of tea.

All at once the lesson I had planned for class that day seemed ridiculous and disconnected from reality, its importance circumvented by the fierce determination of a wounded young girl bent on continuing the journey to save herself. That she had come to a place in her writing where this work must be done regardless of the physical pain it caused spoke volumes to her amazed teacher. And in that moment she indeed became my teacher. Gracie was attending to the wounds of her heart. She was healing herself and her medicine was her words.

Gracie left for good sometime in March of that year. I was never able to find out what happened to her or where she went. She left before I could completely close the gap that our cultures and histories put between us and before I was privy to any of her heart's work—those precious stories of her life. Her empty chair in the pod was a constant reminder of the work she left unfinished.

Her leaving was sudden and I was left to suffer the hollowness of her loss in the quarrelsome wanderings of thoughts. Had I done right by Gracie by encouraging her to write her stories? Was she able to find some measure of peace through her writing? Could she see that she was not completely lost and that she could find her way back? Would she continue to record the rocky journey of her life using the power of her words as a sturdy craft? Had she found in her journal a tool that could help her survive when the world around her took the light away? Maybe so.

And even after many years, I can still recall with musical delight those stolen moments when I first recognized the faintest light of hope and understanding that began to replace some of the dark in my Gracie's eyes. Is she still finding her way down the river of her writing and being? Has the journey she began years ago in her journal made a difference? Has she taken back her life through her stories?

Maybe so.
Yes—Maybe so.

SEVEN

Musings

Storytelling is at the heart of life. As a child, I was never bored because I could always get on with my story. I still love to walk by the water or in the woods listening to the story that never ends. Always my imagination is creating a form that gives shape to otherwise sporadic events in everyday life. Gradually, I am recognizing the meaning of my existence through my own myth. —Marion Woodman (cited by Albert, 1996, p. ix)

People remember the circumstances that profoundly impact their lives—pictures, people, and voices can be recalled in a heartbeat. Time does nothing to tarnish the image. I remember watching Neil Armstrong make history as he offered us "one giant leap for mankind." I remember sitting in the third row, second seat from the window, when Walter Cronkite's news of Dallas filtered into my high school government class. I remember watching the Challenger rattle the ground as it broke the bonds of earth in a perfect liftoff and the surrealistic dance of the explosion that ended its short mission. And I will always remember with crystal clarity the phone call that took me out of my classroom and into the river of my own writing and being.

As I mentioned in the introduction of this book, in the fall of 1988 I was a student in *Writing and Being*. I had only been to the class for two weeks when an event touched my life that would forever change my perspective on what things are truly important. Let me tell you part of the story.

I was in the middle of my third period English class when a fellow teacher came into my room saying I had a phone call in the office—she would stay with my class while I took it. Some sense of foreboding clouded my thoughts as I made my way to the office and picked up the receiver.

In the weeks that followed that phone call, our family life became a kaleidoscope of images with our son Tom at the center of them all. He was desperately ill and would need a very specialized surgery to save his life. Most of my days, from that point on, were a frenetic maze of appointments, tests, procedures, conversations with doctors, and above all, an irrepressible fear that began eating holes in my heart.

One evening I called Lynn Nelson to share the situation and to tell him I would not be in class for a while. I told him I had never known such consuming fear; that it was becoming more and more difficult to make sense of the unfolding events, and that my thinking was crowded with confusion and anger and the hollow feeling of helplessness. Before the conversation was over, Lynn reminded me that there was something I could do that might ease my suffering and help me find the strength to regain my focus—I could use my journal. He told me to write of the struggles going on in my heart—my fears, my pain, and my prayers. He said to write about the anger that was invading my heart and weakening my spirit so that my actions would be driven by a positive force rather that the negativity of despair.

So I began writing a painful chapter of my life story that very night. My journal became the depository of a mother's silent voice. I prayed there, spoke my frustrations and confusion there, and told the blank pages a thousand times, "This isn't fair." I filled line after line with the incoherent ramblings of a soul trying to make sense of an unimaginable situation. And I came to understand the power of my words.

In the end, our son was healed by the miracles of modern medicine but the wounds of my heart found medicine of a different sort: The medicine of writing my story.

I look back to the drama of Tom's illness and my own growing concerns with the direction of education as tributaries that fed into the river of this work. Each challenged my ability to endure the fatigue of difficult situations. Each contained an undercurrent that stirred my emotional insecurities and fed a profound need to seek some form of transformation. Each asked that I realign my thinking to accommodate the complexities of the human spirit. My journal work—my private struggles through troubled waters—became a source of comfort and strength as I began attending to the seedlings that have emerged into this project. The small thoughts and images I planted into the margins of my journal eventually found their way into the form and substance of this work.

In the days when I was just beginning to wonder what contribution I might make to the educational and academic communities, I gave considerable thought to the notions of peace education. I began asking myself what things I could do in my classroom that might change negative behaviors and rekindle a sense of purpose and promise in my students' lives. I wondered about things like the language I used and the way the students and I treated one another. I wondered about the importance of a sense of belonging and being loved, and the consequences of having neither. I wondered about how man's inhumanity toward man seems to be the rule rather than the exception in what we see on television and in the movies. And then one day I looked at the back of the room, and wondered what combination of these things might have caused the dark in Gracie's eyes.

That was probably the defining moment when I realized what I really wanted to do. I wanted to find a way to help Gracie emerge from her cocoon of alienation, to come to a place of personal peace, and to recognize that in her struggles with life she might not be so different from most of us who are learning to find our way. I had been struggling with the abstract idea of peace education and finding it to be too global a concept—too vague for explanation—oddly uncomfortable for some to regard as academically significant. Still, the same words I had come to associate with the notion of peace education would not leave my thoughts: violence, alienation, neglect, guilt, language, spirituality, understanding, and forgiveness. They became nudgings in my mind—always on the ragged hem of the idea.

But the idea for this research had been there all along and had not strayed too far from my original plan. In fact, I believe it to be closely related. Mother Teresa once said that people can do no great things, only "small things with great love." Perhaps this is where great things begin. Could writing the stories of our lives be the first step toward a more global understanding? I realized that by getting my students to tell the stories of their lives I was getting at the very heart of the concepts of peace. The use of narrative storytelling as an instrument of change became the illusive butterfly I finally found in the dark reflection of Gracie's eyes and the contribution I present in this book.

I have jumped into the river of my own writing and being as a result of this research and found myself surprised at some of the meanderings of the water. I share some musings about those surprises here.

Before I began to tell Marcus' story, I was struggling to find a way to present the rich material I was offered. My initial thought was to conduct some sort of dialogue between the respondents and myself, much as I did with Lynn Nelson. I thought that this mode of representation would not only complement the work but would also lend a warmth of authenticity to the project. But this was not to be. This plan became awkward and felt uncomfortable as I began writing. The more I struggled to craft the stories through dialogue and reflection, the more resistant they became.

I remembered Lynn telling his students that they should allow a piece of writing to take whatever form it wanted—to let it emerge naturally. So I began again. This time I did allow the substance of the stories to take its own form. I remember sitting at the computer and watching the screen in amazement as the three life stories unfolded—each like the children in a family, similar in some ways, yet very different in others.

In the end, the stories seemed to take on lives of their own. This time the writing of each felt natural and pleasing. Marcus, Clara, and Maia have only one common facet in their lives—their participation in ENG 494, *Writing and Being.* Like Nelson's poem, it is a "confluence of wonder," three rivers that come together briefly and then branch away again, each following a separate calling.

Another surprise that came on the heels of the form of the stories was the problem of whose voice would do the telling. Writing a life seemed a bit presumptuous of me and I floundered in indecision at the responsibility I was assuming. Do I tell their stories? Should they? Who will be the capital "I" found in the text? Will my experiences taint the honesty and compromise the integrity of the stories?

The more I read about "voice" in the structures of narrative, the more confused I became. The literature is just beginning to attend to the complexities of "voice" in narrative storytelling so opinions on the subject were unconvincing to me. Once again, I had to give up that control and allow the stories to find their own direction. In each story, the "voice" of the respondent emerged naturally and each told his or her own stories. I became the vessel through which the stories could be shared with an audience.

One thing I noticed at the conclusion of this work was the pall of negativity that seemed to blanket most of the stories. This was a curious discovery and quite contrary to the personality characteristics I know of the participants. These are not tragic people. They do not walk about wearing the countenance of gloom. To a person, they are positive, warm, nurturing, and enthusiastic. Our conversations were always charged with laughter and spontaneity.

I wondered about this. Why was there so much suffering and sorrow in the pieces they selected for this study? Where were the stories that made them recall happy times and events? Is there some hidden agenda contained within these stories that has played tricks with my naiveté?

I do not know the answers to these questions. I do know that all of these people sought to heal some part of their lives (hearts) that caused them a sustained pain. They were all hurting from old hidden wounds and needed some catharsis of the spirit if they were to be made well. They all spoke their pain so they did not have to be their pain. They were all a bit like Gracie.

One personal struggle I had during the writing of this project was my usage of language. My vernacular does not approach that which I have read in most other scholarly works. This has, on occasion, caused some concern and embarrassment on my part. On the other hand, what I offer here is reported in the simple honest language that is encouraged in the practice of narrative storytelling. If there *is* a message for the educational community here, I would like it to be told clearly, in the words of my voice, and unfettered by the heady nuances of academic jargon.

As my journey down the river of writing and being comes to an end, I want to revisit my purposes for this research. I have presented the curriculum of a narrative based writing class and its impact on my three respondents for consideration. I have explored the form and substance of narrative storytelling and its possible implications for a writing curriculum through interpretation and reflection. Lastly, I have offered my notions regarding *Narrative Based Evaluation* for contemplation.

This work is for the Gracie in all of us who might bear the weight of a sorrow, struggle with the emptiness of a loss, wrestle with a wound that will not heal—or who like each one of us, just has a story to tell.

Afterword

⌒

I have attempted to show readers who are interested in curriculum alignment a way to look at the philosophical and practical possibilities of storytelling as a tool for program evaluation. This thinking wanders outside traditional constructs of a culture comfortable (or at least somewhat comfortable) with left-brained educational objectives, standardized testing, and quantitative assessment. To many this book represents thinking that may indeed be very uncomfortable—even suspect—in terms of its simplistic message and timeless necessity. This book is about writing and sharing stories as part of an authentic system for evaluation. Those in positions to deny its validity and overlook its promise might do so. Some will not. Some will think about a curriculum that wraps itself around storytelling as a way for all of us to nudge a little closer to personal revelation and understanding. What then? Could these first steps of personal transformation act like a small stone tossed into a glassy lake, birthing circle after circle until . . . well, maybe until our turbulent society can begin to feel its gentle strength?

Throughout this book I have used the metaphor of light, relating it to critical thinking in the theory that perhaps we should hold new approaches in educational thought up to the light to see what shines through—allow these new approaches to not only catch the sun but fraction themselves into the vibrant colors of possibility. If we are willing to take a step outside the boundaries of traditional curricular design just a little, if we can reclaim one of our most sacred possession—the stories of our lives—then maybe we can come to think of *Narrative Based Evaluation* as wording toward the light.

Bibliography

Albert, S. W. (1996). *Writing from life: Telling your soul's story.* New York: G. P. Putnam's Sons.

Apple, M. (1990). *Ideology and curriculum.* New York: Routledge, Chapman and Hall.

Bal, M. (1991). *On story-telling.* Sonoma, CA: Polebridge Press.

Barone, T. (1992a). Beyond theory and method: A case for critical storytelling. *Theory into Practice, 31*(2), 142–146.

Barone, T. (1992b). The demise of subjectivity in educational inquiry. *Curriculum Inquiry, 22*(2), 25–38.

Barone, T. (1993). Breaking the mold: The new American student as strong poet. *Theory Into Practice, 32*(4), 236–242.

Barone, T. (1995). Persuasive writings, vigilant readings, and constructed characters: The paradox of trust in educational storytelling. *Qualitative Studies in Education, 8*(1), 63–72.

Barone, T. (1997). Among the chosen: A collaborative educational (auto)biography. *Qualitative Inquiry, 3*(2), 222–235.

Barone, T., & Eisner, E. (1997). Arts-based educational research. In Richard M. Jaeger (Ed.), *Complementary methods for research in education* (2nd ed., pp. 71–116). Washington, DC: American Educational Research Association.

Bey, T. M., & Turner, G. (1996). *Making school a place of peace.* Thousand Oaks, CA: Corwin Press.

Bloom, B. S. (1971). *The handbook of formative and summative evaluation.* New York: McGaw-Hill.

Bourdieu, P. (1993). *Outline of a theory of practice.* Cambridge, MA: Harvard University Press.

Bruner, J. (1986). *Actual minds, possible worlds.* Cambridge, MA: Harvard University Press.

Bruner, J. (1990). *Acts of meaning.* Cambridge, MA: Harvard University Press.

Bryk, A. S. (Ed.). (1983). *Stakeholder-based evaluation.* San Francisco: Jossey-Bass.

Bucher, C. J. (1990). *Three models on a rocking horse: A comparative study in narratology.* Bonn, Germany: Gunter Narr Verlag.

Carter, J. (1995a). *Always a reckoning.* New York: Times Books.

Carter, J. (1995b). *Talking peace.* New York: Puffin Books.

Carter, K. (1993). *The place of story in the study of teaching and teacher education.* Oklahoma City, OK: Custom Academic Publishing.

Cather, K. D. (1924). *Educating my story-telling.* New York: World Book.

Cleaver, E. (1968). *Soul on ice.* New York: Dell Publishing.

Connelly, F. M., & Clandinin, P. J. (1987). *Narrative, experience, and the study of curriculum.* Washington, DC: The American Association of Colleges for Teacher Education.

Connelly, F. M., & Clandinin, P. J. (1988). Studying teachers' knowledge of classrooms: Collaborative research, ethics, and the negotiation of narrative. *The Journal of Educational Thought, 21*(3), 130–139.

Connelly, F. M., & Clandinin, P. J. (1990). Stories experience and narrative inquiry. *Educational Researcher, 19*(5), 2–14.

Connelly, F. M., & Clandinin, P. J. (1991). Narrative inquiry: Storied experience. In E. Short (Ed.), *Forms of curriculum inquiry* (pp. 121–154). Albany: State University of New York Press.

Cortazzi, M. (1993). *Narrative analysis.* London: The Falmer Press.

Cruikshank, J. (1990). *Life lived like a story.* Lincoln: University of Nebraska Press.

Czarniawska, B. (1998). *A narrative approach to organization studies.* Thousand Oaks, CA: Sage Publications.

Denzin, N., & Lincoln, Y. (1994). *Handbook of qualitative research.* Thousand Oaks, CA: Sage Publications.

Dyson, A. H., & Genishi, C. (Eds.). (1994). *The need for story: Cultural diversity in classroom and community.* Urbana, IL: National Council of Teachers of English.

Eeds, M., & Peterson, R. (1997). Literature studies revisited: Some thoughts on talking to children about books. *The New Advocate, 10*(1), 49–59.

Egan, K. (1988). *Teaching as story telling.* London: Routledge.

Eisner, E. W. (1985a). *The art of educational evaluation: A personal view.* Philadelphia: Falmer Press.

Eisner, E. W. (1985b). *The educational imagination: On the design and evaluation of school programs.* New York: Macmillan.

Eisner, E., & Peshkin, A. (Eds.). (1990). *Qualitative inquiry in education: The continuing debate.* New York: Teachers College Press.

Evans, E., & Cocoran, B. (1987). *Readers, texts, teachers.* Monclair, CA: Open University Press.

Fludernik, M. (1996). *Towards a "natural" narratology.* London: Routledge.

Freire, P. (1994). *Pedagogy of the oppressed.* New York: Continuum.

Freund, E. (1987). *The return of the reader: Reader response criticism.* London: Methuen.

Gore, J. (1993). *The struggle for pedagogies.* New York: Routledge.

Greene, M. (1991). Foreword. In C. Witherell & N. Noddings (Eds.), *Stories lives tell* (p. ix). New York: Teachers College Press.

Griffith, K. (2001). *Searching for light: Finding voices of pride through narrative and poetic expression.* Unpublished doctoral dissertation, Arizona State University, Tempe.

Guba, E., & Lincoln, Y. (1989). *Fourth generation evaluation.* Newbury Park, CA: Sage Publications.

Haggerson, N. (1971). *To dance with joy.* New York: Exposition Press.

Haggerson, N. (1993). *from Geronimo's lookout.* Tempe, AZ: Nornel Associates.

Haggerson, N., & Bowman, A. (1992). *Informing educational policy and practice through interpretive inquiry.* Lancaster, PA: Technomic Publishing.

Harrison, M. (1995). *Ann Lee: The sustaining medicine of her stories. A case study.* Unpublished thesis, Arizona State University, Tempe.

Harrison, M. (1999). Writing and being: The transformational power of storytelling reported through narrative based evaluation. *Dissertation Abstracts International, 60*(03A), 636. (University Microfilms No. AA19923935)

Hatch, J. A., & Wisniewski, R. (Eds.). (1995). *Life history and narrative.* London: Falmer Press.

Hirsch, E. D. (1976). *The aims of interpretation.* Chicago: University of Chicago Press.

Hogan, L. (1995). *Dwellings.* New York: W. W. Norton.

Holland, K. (1993). *Journeying.* Portsmouth, NH: Heinemann.

hooks, b. (1992). *Narratives of struggle.* Boston, MA: South End Press.

Hopkins, R. (1994). *Toward narrative schooling.* New York: Teachers College Press.

Horton, M., & Freire, P. (1990). *We make the road by walking: Conversations on educational and social change.* Philadelphia: Temple University Press.

House, E. R. (1986). *New directions in educational evaluation.* London: Falmer Press.

International thesaurus of quotation. (1970). Rhonda Thomas Tripp, Compiler. New York: Harper and Row.

Iser, W. (1974). *Implied reader.* Baltimore: Johns Hopkins University Press.

Josselson, R., & Lieblich, A. (Eds.). (1993). *The narrative study of lives.* Newbury Park, CA: Sage Publications.

Karolides, N. (1992). *Reader response in the classroom.* New York: Longman.

Keen, S., & Fox, A. V. (1973). *Telling your story.* New York: Doubleday.

Kemmis, S., & McTaggart, R. (1981). *The action research planner.* Victoria, Australia: Deakin University.

Kiesinger, C. E. (1998). From interview to story: Writing Abbie's life. *Qualitative Inquiry, 1*(4), 71–93.

Kopp, S. (1976). *If you meet the Buddha on the road, kill him.* Toronto, Canada: Bantam Books.

Kozol, J. (1992). *Savage inequalities.* New York: Harper Collins.

Lather, P. (1991). *Getting smart: Feminist research and pedagogy within the postmodern.* New York: Routledge.

Lincoln, Y., & Guba, E. (1995). *Naturalistic inquiry.* Beverly Hills, CA: Sage Publications.

Linde, C. (1993). *Life stories.* New York: Oxford University Press.

Lopez, B. (1987). *Arctic dreams.* New York: Vintage.

McEwan, H., & Egan, K. (1995). *Narrative in teaching, learning, and research.* New York: Teachers College Press.

Migotsky, C., Stake, R., Davis, R., Williams, B., DePaul, G., Cisnernos, E. J., Johnson, E., & Feltovich, J. (1997). Probative, dialectic, and moral reasoning in program evaluation. *Qualitative Inquiry, 3*(2), 453–465. Thousand Oaks, CA: Sage Publications.

Miller, B. (1980). *Teaching the art of literature.* Urbana, IL: National Council of Teachers of English.

Moustakas, C. (1990). *Heuristic research.* Thousand Oaks, CA: Sage Publications.

Munro, P. (1993). Continuing dilemmas of life history research: A reflexive attempt of feminist qualitative inquiry. In D. Flinders & G. Mills (Eds.), *Theory and concepts of qualitative research: Perspectives in the field* (pp. 163–167). New York: Teachers College Press.

Murray, D. M. (1996). *Crafting a life: In essay, story, poem.* Portsmouth, NH: Heinemann.

Nash, C. (Ed.). (1990). *Narrative in culture: The uses of storytelling in the sciences, philosophy, and literature.* London: Routledge.

Nelson, G. L. (1994). *Writing and being: Taking back our lives through the power of language.* San Diego: Lura Media.

Nelson, G. L. (2000). Warriors with words: Toward a post-Columbine writing curriculum. *English Journal, 89*(5), 9–13.

Noddings, N. (1992). *The challenge to care in schools.* New York: Teachers College Press.

Nye, E. S. (1997). Writing as healing. *Qualitative Inquiry, 3*(4), 439–452.

O'Reilley, M. R. (1993). *The peaceable classroom.* Portsmouth, NH: Boynton/Cook Publishers.

PDK National Study Committee on Evaluation. (1971). *Educational evaluation and decision making.* Itaska, IL: F. E. Peacock Publishers.

Peterson, R., & Eeds, M. (1990). *Grand conversations: Literature study groups in action.* Ontario, Canada: Scholastic-TAB.

Pinar, W., Reynolds, W., Slattery, P., & Taubman, P. (1995). *Understanding curriculum.* New York: Peter Lang.

Popham, W. J. (1975). *Educational evaluation.* Englewood Cliffs, NJ: Prentice-Hall.

Pradl, G. (1984). *Narratology: The study of story structure.* Urbana, IL: ERIC Clearinghouse on Reading and Communication Skills. (ERIC Document Reproduction Service No. ED 250698)

Progoff, I. (1992). *At a journal workshop.* New York: G. P. Putman's Sons.

Purpel, D. (1989). *The moral and spiritual crises in education.* New York: Bergin and Garvey.

Random House Webster's college dictionary. (1992). New York: Random House.

Riessman, C. K. (1993). *Narrative analysis.* Newbury Park, CA: Sage Publications.

Schwab, J. (1964). The structure of disciplines: Meanings and significances. In G. W. Ford & L. Pugo (Eds.), *The structure of knowledge and the curriculum* (pp. 1-30). Chicago, IL: Rand-McNally.

Scriven, M. (1967). *The methodology of evaluation.* Paper presented at the annual meeting of the American Research Association, Chicago.

Scriven, M. (1973). Goal-free evaluation. In E. R. House (Ed.), *School evaluation: The politics and process* (pp. 319–328). Berkeley, CA: McCutchan.

Scriven, M. (1983). Evaluation ideologies. In G. F. Madaus, M. S. Scriven, & D. L. Stuffelbeam (Eds.), *Evaluation models* (pp. 229–260). Boston: Kluwer-Nijhoff.

Scriven, M. (1987). Validity in personnel evaluation. *Journal of Personnel Evaluation, 1*(1), 9–24.

Shafer, R. (1992). *Retelling a life: Narration and dialogue in psychoanalysis.* New York: Basic Books.

Short, E. (Ed.). (1991). *Forms of curriculum inquiry.* Albany: State University of New York Press.

Spore, M. B. (1997). *A way to travel through the human heart: Fiction in educational research.* Paper presented at the annual meeting of the American Educational Research Association, Chicago.

Stake, R. E. (1967). *The countenance of educational evaluation.* New York: Teachers College Record.

Stock, P. L. (1995). *The dialogic curriculum.* Portsmouth, NH: Heinemann.

Strauss, A., & Corbin, J. (1990). *Basics of qualitative research.* London: Sage Publications.

Tompkins, G. (1993). *Teaching reading with literature.* New York: Macmillan.

Tyler, R. W. (1969). *Educational evaluation: New roles, new means.* Chicago: University of Chicago Press.

Wanner, S. (1994). *On with the story.* Portsmouth, NH: Heinemann.

Weiler, K. (1988). *Women teaching for change.* New York: Begin and Garvey.

Wilhelm, J. D. (1995). *"You gotta be the book"* (pp. xi–19). New York: Teachers College Press.

Williams, T. T. (1994). *An unspoken hunger: Stories from the field.* New York: Pantheon Books.

Witherell, C., & Noddings, N. (1991). *Stories lives tell.* New York: Teachers College Press.

Studies in the Postmodern Theory of Education

General Editors
Joe L. Kincheloe & Shirley R. Steinberg

Counterpoints publishes the most compelling and imaginative books being written in education today. Grounded on the theoretical advances in criticalism, feminism, and postmodernism in the last two decades of the twentieth century, Counterpoints engages the meaning of these innovations in various forms of educational expression. Committed to the proposition that theoretical literature should be accessible to a variety of audiences, the series insists that its authors avoid esoteric and jargonistic languages that transform educational scholarship into an elite discourse for the initiated. Scholarly work matters only to the degree it affects consciousness and practice at multiple sites. Counterpoints' editorial policy is based on these principles and the ability of scholars to break new ground, to open new conversations, to go where educators have never gone before.

For additional information about this series or for the submission of manuscripts, please contact:

Joe L. Kincheloe & Shirley R. Steinberg
c/o Peter Lang Publishing, Inc.
275 Seventh Avenue, 28th floor
New York, New York 10001

To order other books in this series, please contact our Customer Service Department:

(800) 770-LANG (within the U.S.)
(212) 647-7706 (outside the U.S.)
(212) 647-7707 FAX

Or browse online by series:
www.peterlangusa.com